Winning
is not enough

Winning
is not enough

Sports stars who are going for gold — and God

Andrew Wingfield Digby
Stuart Weir
Foreword by Gerald Williams

MarshallPickering
An Imprint of HarperCollinsPublishers

First published in Great Britain in 1991
by Marshall Pickering

Marshall Pickering is an imprint of
HarperCollinsReligious,
Part of HarperCollinsPublishers
77–85 Fulham Palace Road
Hammersmith, London W6 8JB

Printed and bound in Great Britain by
HarperCollins Book Manufacturing, Glasgow

A catalogue record for this book
is available from the British Library

For our families
Sue, Anna, Mark and Laura Wingfield Digby
Lynne, Christine and Jonathan Weir

CONTENTS

Acknowledgements

The authors wish to thank a number of people who have helped with the preparation of this book.

First of all our thanks to the sportspeople who are featured. We are grateful to

> Kriss and Monika Akabusi
> Garth and Funkazi Crooks
> Graham and Kathy Davies
> Kitrina Douglas
> Jonathan and Alison Edwards
> Mikie Heaton-Ellis
> Brian and Donna Irvine
> Alan and Jan Knott
> Bernhard and Vikki Langer
> Lisa Opie

for their willingness in giving us of their time and for their patience and honesty in answering what must have seemed interminable questions.

We are grateful for the assistance of Marzena Bogdanowicz, Press Officer of the Squash Rackets Association, Ian McKenzie, Editor of *Squash Player International* and the Rev. Bruce Gillingham for assistance in various ways. We acknowledge our gratitude to Bridgette Lawrence for allowing us to draw heavily on her appreciation of Wilf Slack (see bibliography).

Thanks, too, to our secretaries, Joy Williams and Helen Nunn, who typed much of the manuscript.

Our thanks to all those Christians involved in sport who support our work financially and pray for us, thus enabling us to do jobs we love. We both long that the Christian presence in every level of sport will grow more and more, and in that spirit we offer you the book.

FOREWORD

How do you like this quote: "A big shot on his knees isn't any taller than anyone else!"

I'd like to be able to claim it as my own, but these are the words of A. W. Tozer. And I treasure them.

Yet why do we offer centre stage to big-shot Christians? Answer: because Jesus said, "Go and make disciples of all nations" (Matthew 28:19). It was His great commission. And if we are serious about following Him, we have to explain the Gospel of Christ in everyday language and use every God-given means possible to make the people out there sit up and listen.

One way – one of many – is to use big-shot Christians; and that includes big-shot sportsmen who are followers of Jesus. Young people, especially, will come to hear pop singers and sporting heroes.

And so the people my friends Andrew Wingfield Digby and Stuart Weir have written about in this book, and many other sporting celebrities like Margaret Court and Stan Smith (from my particular game), have a platform from which to speak out the greatest truth we will ever hear, a platform that scores of noble preachers would give their right hand to possess.

It was after spending just over a week in the company of 150 famous Christian sportsmen and women, and discovering that it was possible to be "religious" and also lead an exciting and adventurous life, that I, for one, had my eyes opened, so I speak from personal experience.

I'm prejudiced: I'm a devoted sporting buff. I belief that one of the most fundamental blessings of God is the ability to run – just that. But there are two other reasons why I so gladly involve myself among Christians in the family of sport.

The first is this. To succeed in sport, above all, you have to be committed. What lifts the best five tennis players in the world above a hundred or so of their challenging peers is their total commitment. And so to speak to sportsmen and women is to speak not to wimps and don't-knows but to people of ambition and vision and dedication. They're not afraid to go for it. They don't hide in the grey anonymity of the also-rans.

So it doesn't surprise me that, when the Good News of Jesus Christ is presented in an unequivocal and relevant manner by people who themselves are attractive and successful, "normal" and not "preachy", there is a marked response.

Demonstrate to them, by example, that Jesus changes and energises lives, that He is a *living* force, and that in Him – and Him only – are the answers to their questions, and many will commit themselves to Him and be His people on the sporting field.

The second reason for my belief in the work of "Christians in Sport" is that sportsmen and women at the top class discover at a far younger age than the rest of us an absolutely fundamental truth.

That truth is this: that the moment of mountain-top experience that we believe will sustain us for life – the winning goal at the Cup Final, the crucial try at Twickenham, the sublime century at Lord's, the crashing ace that clinches a Wimbledon championship – that heady delight *lasts only a very short time*. Very short indeed.

Like Charles Duke, the astronaut who stepped on the

face of the moon (can you think of any achievement more apocalyptic?), all too soon you find yourself asking: What next? What next to fill the emptiness?

That void is part of God's plan in creation. He left it there when He made Man. It is the place He wants to occupy. And nothing else – no amout of wealth or success – can fill that God-shaped hole in each one of us.

Most of us discover that truth late in life because we tend to scale our personal summit in our forties and fifties, which is why that age is so often a time of deep questioning and, perhaps, disenchantment.

Our sporting heroes discover this at the peak of their young lives. There's nothing, I promise you, more empty and aimless than yesterday's faded and crumpled headliners, stripped of the buttress of acclaim. Watch them swallow their sad g-and-t's.

Jesus came that we might have fulness. *All* our lives.

Gerald Williams
The Millmead Centre
Guildford

INTRODUCTION

By highlighting the lives of the people featured in this book, we are aware that we are putting them under pressure. There have been those in the past who have made a very public confession of their Christian faith, only to fall away from it subsequently. This has been very painful for us and very traumatic and sad for them. Often, of course, people's faith is renewed later on in their lives.

In describing the careers and priorities of the people featured in this book we are under no illusions. They are imperfect, just as we are who wrote the book. They struggle to maintain Christian standards in and out of their sport. They, like us, are constantly assessing and thinking through the challenge of the Gospel to their lifestyle. They, like us, depend entirely on God's goodness to keep going at all.

The truth of the Christian faith does not depend on the integrity of those who profess it. Obviously it is very helpful when Christians consistently practise what they preach. But the claims of Christianity are true or untrue regardless of how we live. Either Jesus of Nazareth was the Son of God, who died so that we can be forgiven and rose again as our trailblazer into eternity, or He was not. Either He will return one day as King or He will not. What a professional footballer in England, or a West Indian cricketer or a German golfer believes has no bearing on the facts of Christianity. About those all of us must make up our own minds.

We have no way of knowing what the subjects of this book will believe in one, ten, twenty or fifty years. What we have tried to describe here is what they say now, and what we hope and pray they will be saying when they finally come face to face with God as we all must. We, ourselves, are quite convinced that what the Bible teaches, what may broadly be called the Christian world view, is true and right. We have found it to be relevant and applicable to our own lives.

In these eleven chapters the reader will meet men and women who have similarly been convinced. They like us have had varying levels of success in applying their faith to their lives. Like us, they would want to say that a personal commitment to Jesus is not only the best way to live, it is also the most rewarding and the most exciting.

In the world of sport it can also be, at times, very hard. But it is possible, we most definitely want to affirm, to be a Christian in sport.

KRISS AKABUSI

"Where's 'Arry, then?"

Big Frank Bruno was going through his full repertoire of post-match clichés. The man with the big grin sitting beside me was screaming with laughter. Occasionally he would look up, see who was in the room and shout, "Come and see this, come and see this, come and see this!" Kriss Akabusi has a way of saying the same thing several times at breakneck speed when he is enjoying himself.

We were sitting in the coffee bar in the athletes' village at the 1986 Commonwealth Games in Edinburgh. I was just a spare part – an assistant to the chaplain's assistant or some such title. Boredom is one of the biggest problems for athletes at these great sports festivals, so there was a big TV screen in the corner of the room. It was Frank Bruno's latest "epic" that had drawn Kriss and me together. He certainly had no idea who I was, and to be honest I wasn't quite sure which of the British athletes he was! We laughed together and passed the time of day – I knew nothing of the life-changing events going on in Kriss's mind and heart during those games.

Kriss Kezie Uche Chukwu Duru-Akabusi, was born on 28th November 1958, in Paddington, London. When he was three he suffered the same fate as the famous bear, and was abandoned by his Nigerian parents who had to return to their war-torn country. Kriss spent the next few years with various foster parents in different places before being sent at the tender age of eight years to a children's home in Enfield, north London.

These were not very happy days for the extrovert athletic youngster, for while he was never lacking for material comforts, he received precious little intimacy or affection. He has a quick and intelligent mind, so his academic failure to secure any O-levels speaks volumes for the traumas of his childhood. It was a desire for security and a career that took the institutionalised, rootless teenager to the all-consuming embrace of the British Army.

He had already shown all-round athletic ability, enjoying the gladiatorial aspects of football and basketball. In athletics he had excelled only in the high jump and then to no exciting degree. But perhaps this talent presaged the crucial decision years later to switch from 400 metres flat to the rigorous hurdles events at which he has made his name. The army offered continued institutional life, a family, a uniform, a wage packet and a career. It also, crucially for Kriss and the future of British athletics, offered physical fitness.

In the Royal Signals he excelled at the team sports and in his first summer as a 17-year-old won his first championship – a 400-metre race for his unit. Kriss took life as it came in the army, and had little thought in his early days either for God or a career in world class athletics. But he was learning vital lessons which were to have a great importance in turning the gangly teenager into a champion. Principally he was learning about discipline and self-control. Four hundred metre hurdling requires a vital combination of speed, strength and technique. The hurdler who can hold himself together technically under physical pressure is at a great advantage. Akabusi learnt about this in the army. He was posted to West Germany, where a very attractive blonde gymnastics and ballet student called Monika attracted his attention. Monika took Kriss to the athletics club at Gutersloh. A little Teutonic order was introduced into the chaos of his unruly running style.

In due course Kriss and Monika were married and she has remained a vital support and encouragement to him throughout his career. Marriage to a top-class athlete in any sport is not easy. There are long periods away from home, anti-social hours, piles of washing and ironing, constant telephone calls and more than the ordinary financial worries. An athlete can be earning a sizable income for a few years but with very limited long-term prospects. It is easy for a partner to get used to a standard of living which is unsustainable when the athlete's competitive career is over.

Coupled to this, all great champions (that I have met, anyway) are egoists. There has to be self-belief and almost ruthless determination. You don't get to the top if you are constantly thinking of the other person. Marriage requires a great deal of give and take, and the sacrifices required to be a successful husband don't come naturally to the athlete who is being urged by his coach to "dig deep" and "hang tough". Monika has not had an easy time, and it has been made worse by Kriss's conversion to Christianity. The man is a world champion enthusiast and does nothing by halves.

At the time of writing she does not share his faith. She is embarrassed and a little hurt by his eagerness to shout about Jesus from the rooftops. She also feels he is vulnerable, and is too easily "used" by Christians as a speaker or a celebrity. He finds it very hard to say "no" to the numerous invitations he receives, and some of those who ring simply will not take "no" for an answer.

One journalist asked Kriss to support an appeal for a

local hospital. Kriss knew he did not have time to do it properly and rightly said he would not get involved. "I thought you were a Christian!" came the reply. Monika resents this treatment of her husband.

"You Christians must be careful how you treat us non-Christians", she told me, voicing her feeling that she is often disregarded by those who, as she sees it, are manipulating Kriss.

There is nothing Kriss likes more than telling people about Jesus whenever he can at church functions. There's nothing Monika likes less. She has learnt to cope with the adulation of athletics fans queuing for her husband's autograph and lionising him wherever he goes. But being a Christian "superstar" was an altogether different thing. Kriss is finding that being a Christian husband is every bit as difficult as winning an Olympic gold medal, but is a lot more important.

Monika acknowledges gladly that becoming a Christian has made Kriss a more loving and caring husband and father. "He certainly gives us more time and attention," she says, "but he is very different to when I married him, and I find it very difficult." They both acknowledge that if they had met after he had become a Christian they would never have got married.

"Sometimes," Kriss says, "people think that being a Christian solves all your problems, but I will tell you it creates a few, too." As many people find in this situation, there is a real gulf between them, but they are very honest with each other and have every intention of working at their relationship and sticking together.

For the moment, though, let's return to the athletics career of one of Britain's most popular sportsmen. At LG Gutersloh Hansi Bohme, a top German coach, saw Kriss's potential and began to work with him. Bohme weaned his protégé off football and basketball and got him to concentrate on the one-lap race. By 1980 he was winning races in Germany and clocking 48 seconds – only half decent, but he was on his way.

A key moment came when he decided to transfer from the Royal Signals to the Army Physical Training Corps. This involved a return to England where he attended a coaching course at which Mike Smith, an excellent track coach, spoke. Kriss joined Mike's squad of runners which included Todd Bennett in Southampton and the fairy tale began.

To the technical improvement Kriss had made in Germany, Smith added mental and physical toughness. One short winter passed and in the summer of 1983 the big jump into world class athletics took place. Kriss ran 46.10 that summer and came second in the UK Championships to Alan Slack. He was selected for the Great Britain team against the USSR and still remembers rushing home with his selection letter from Frank Dick. He had arrived in the big time.

The story of Kriss's career as a 400 metre runner on the flat is strangely unfulfilling. He was a late starter, but within a year of top class competition was standing on the Olympic rostrum in Los Angeles receiving a silver medal for the relay. He captained the England team against the USA in 1985, and in 1986 struck gold in the relay at the Commonwealth Games. But he had slipped to number five in the country having been number three. He only travelled as a reserve in the relay squad to the European Championships, and ran, winning another gold medal, only because his great friend Bennett was injured.

To understand Akabusi correctly we have to get to his mental state around this time. He was about to make two vital decisions which changed the whole of his life. He switched from flat to hurdles, and he became a Christian.

Kriss tends to tell Christian audiences that 1986 was the time that he began to be interested in Christianity. When he got to Edinburgh he found a Good News Bible in his room – a special edition incidentally, produced by the National Bible Society of Scotland and presented to all competitors at the Games. Kriss says, ''I read the whole lot while I was in Edinburgh because I was so spiritually hungry.'' This was his condition as we laughed ourselves silly at the Frank Bruno interview.

But in an article in *Athletics Today* Kriss's emphasis is a mixture of patriotic fervour and personal ambition. ''In Edinburgh I reflected on what event I could represent my country at, and as the 400, 800 and 400 metre hurdles went by I considered my options. The first two were out, with Roger Black reigning supreme, while the 800 talent with a 1, 2, 3 was awesome – I made up my mind to have a go at the hurdles at which no Briton had got past the first round.''

So what was the pre-Christian, pre-hurdles Akabusi really like? Crucial elements in his make-up, produced no doubt by his disjointed and lonely childhood, were his longing for security and his love of competition and winning. He had found security in the army and his happy relationship with Monika. He had lived in the fast lane of life, too; he was usually to the fore when it came to the partying and discoing after athletics meetings. His past life, without being conspicuously wild, would certainly have interested the tabloids. And he had got used to winning. He won his inter-services races, he won for his club, and he had become a winner for his country. Yet he knew he could not be the best in the country at 400 metres. The first of two daughters, Ashanti and Shakira, had arrived. Suddenly both security and winning were less guaranteed than they had been. It would be wrong to think of the 1986 Akabusi as in crisis, but he was thinking very hard about the direction of his life and what was most important.

An indication of the importance of Kriss's faith can be gauged from the fact that from 1986 onwards it is impossible to divorce the hurdling Akabusi from the Christian Akabusi. Before 1986 Kriss had had a materialistic view of life. From the earliest days he had thought that he must gather around him as many toys as possible: fast cars, a nice home, a good music system. The purpose of life, he thought, was to die with as many "things" as possible. The way to acquire them was through fame and success. And by and large he succeeded. He had a nice car in his garage, a detached home, and an Olympic silver medal in the cupboard, and yet he found himself constantly longing for more.

His attitude to his cars reveals his values. Before 1986 he would change his car constantly. When he eventually fulfilled his great ambition to own a Mercedes, he was driving flat out on the motorway when he was overtaken by someone in a bigger one. "No sooner than I'd got something, there was something else I wanted. I began to think that there had to be another meaning to life."

It says a great deal for what happened that for the next four years he didn't change his car at all!

In the Good News New Testament in Edinburgh, Kriss read about a man, the like of whom he had never encountered before. This was a man with power. He healed the incurably ill, walked on water, multiplied food, and even raised the dead. This was a man who was popular. Huge crowds followed him wherever He went. This was a man who was brave. He fearlessly criticised the religious establishment and calmly faced His Roman executioners. This was a man who was tough and yet gentle. He loved little children to come to Him and was unendingly patient with His wayward followers. This was a man whose teaching was compelling. Sergeant Akabusi was expected to love his enemies. This Jesus of whom he was reading was a man who made sacrifices. He believed in His mission so completely that He gave up all home comforts, family and personal ambition to fulfil it. This was a man who was prepared to die. As he read, Kriss saw that Jesus deliberately headed for Jerusalem where he was certain to die on a Roman cross. And yet, he saw that this was a man who convinced His followers that He overcame death. So surely were they persuaded that the direction of their lives was changed for ever.

Kriss was fascinated by it. He knew that he had to find out if all that he read was true. It took him ten months of searching to be convinced. He examined the evidence for the Resurrection. He looked up references to Jesus and early Christianity in contemporary Roman and Jewish writers like Tacitus and Josephus. In so far as he could without any formal theological training, he checked it all out to see if it would hold water. He was satisfied . . . almost.

One final, almost bizarre consideration finally persuaded him that he must follow this Jesus. He observed that his birthday was on 28th November, 1958. It struck him as truly amazing that his birthday should be dated from the coming of Jesus. The entire calendar was determined and rearranged by an obscure carpenter from Nazareth. As Kriss would put it, "Jesus had to be the main man!"

He was training in America when he met the Lord. For months he had been nearly ready to make his decision, and one night he simply prayed: "Lord, if you are there, and I really don't know if you are, you'd better come and say 'Hi' to Kriss." And he did. Kriss became clearly aware of Jesus with him. Whether it was a vision, or simply a growing awareness, he's not sure; but he does know that from that night on he was certain that he was a Christian, and that he had entered into a relationship which was totally real now and would last beyond death and forever. That conviction has not changed since.

Next morning he rushed up to Daley Thompson and Edwin Moses at training and burst out, "Hey, guys, I met Jesus last night!" Apparently they exchanged knowing looks! When he returned from the States in the summer of 1987 he got involved in a church in Southampton, and also with Christians in Sport. His Christian growth, which was to be remarkably rapid, had begun.

What also began was a phenomenally successful career in 400 metre hurdling.

It all began very inauspiciously. He did some preparatory work in Manchester with the national coach, Peter Warden, and trained with Max Robertson who was one of his new rivals. But it was Mike Whittingham, who had run fourth in the 1982 Commonwealth Games, who helped him most. Out in California, Thompson and Moses also offered him their advice. Since Thompson was the greatest decathlete of all time and Moses a living legend at 400 metre hurdles, Akabusi was getting a privileged education. Perhaps he was overconfident in his first race because he ended it flat on his face after hitting the eighth hurdle! Two days after returning to England he had to run at Reading in order to qualify for the UK championships at Derby. Despite "making a real mess of half the hurdles" he clocked 51.9 and got into the meet. Incredibly he ran 49.56 to dead heat with Robertson. Everyone knew that he had the basic speed, but at hurdles that is not enough.

Kriss is unstinting in his praise of Mike Whittingham who was "the fundamental ingredient in sorting out my technique and has remained so". Together they worked out a four-year plan which would culminate in a gold medal at the 1990 European Championships and a medal place at the World Championships in Tokyo in 1991, taking in a Commonwealth gold in Auckland on the way. 1992 means the Olympic Games in Barcelona, and a real rush at the magic gold medal that everyone in British athletics remembers David Hemery winning in Mexico in 1968.

Most plans of this kind have to be adjusted seasonally, but so far Kriss's and Mike's has run like clockwork. It reads like Roy of the Rovers. When David Coleman read out the list of his achievements while introducing him to viewers of the BBC quiz show "A Question of Sport" in November 1990, Kriss's grin got broader and broader.

In the World Championships in 1987 the novice Akabusi came seventh in 48.64. In Seoul at the Olympics he was the leading European as he ran sixth in the final in 48.69. Next came his epic and inspiring 48.95 to win the first race of the Europa Cup at Gateshead which set up an historic British win and entry into the World Cup in Barcelona where he won the Bronze medal. In January 1990 he collected the Commonwealth gold in Auckland, and it all culminated in the 47.92 to win the European Championships in Split and bust David Hemery's 22-year-old record. This made Akabusi number 3 in the world.

Behind each one of these great performances there is a story of Christian witness, rigorous training and plenty of laughs.

Before the track and field athletes arrived in Seoul they spent time in a training camp in Japan. Already attempts had been made to get the Christians in the team together, but in Japan by their own initiative the "fellowship meetings" took off. The leading lights, apart from Kriss, were long jumper Barrington Williams and triple jumpers Jonathan Edwards and Vernon Samuels. They were joined by others. Derek Redmond, the 400 metre UK record holder, and Judy Simpson, our finest heptathlete, would trace the beginnings of their Christian lives to these meetings. At a final day communion service about 17 of the British track and field team gathered together to sing, pray and study the Bible together.

Over the water in Korea Peter Swaffield and I were anxiously awaiting the belated arrival of the English athletes. We were two of a team of 28 international chaplains working alongside 30 or so Koreans in the unhelpfully named "Protestant Chapel". We had planned daily services and Bible studies and were looking forward to the support of the Christians in the British team. They came very late – a day after the official opening ceremony – but imagine our delight when we discovered that they had initiated meetings themselves.

"Yes," said Akabusi, "we certainly want to meet every day . . . but let's do it out in the open so that everyone knows and can join us if they want to." Such an initiative from the chaplains would have been frowned on by the Games Committee, but as it was the athletes' idea there was no problem.

Each evening around 6pm we would gather on the flag plaza of the Village. Jonathan Edwards or Peter Swaffield had a guitar, many had Bibles. It became a great gathering of Christians and interested enquirers from all over the world – and on occasions it was conducted in the full blaze of the world's TV cameras. Kriss would lead with his friend and training partner from Nigeria, Innocent Egbunike. All the athletes would introduce themselves, and at the end Innocent would say, "Well, thank you, brothers, but I only am innocent!"

On one occasion, Kriss asked each person what needs

they had for prayer. It was the night before the final of the 4×400 metres, and three of the finalists were present – Danny Harris from the USA team, Egbunike and Akabusi. I remember we prayed for various people. One wanted to find other Christians in her team, Kriss was concerned about a hamstring injury, Judy asked that she would be more committed. We all looked expectantly to Innocent. "I don't ask that I should win, Lord," he said, "but please, please don't let me finish behind Akabusi." The meeting ended in chaotic laughter.

The winter of 88–89 was a period of intensive training for Kriss. Again he went to America, and got involved in a strong Bible teaching church in California. The Bible has always been very important in Akabusi's life. To hear him speak you would think he had learnt most of it off by heart! He has a great hunger to know about God, and when he eventually left the Army in the autumn of 1990 it was to combine his training in the US with a course in theology and secular philosophy.

The 1989 season saw continued advance. He did his best time, 48.92, and played a full part in the triumphs in Gateshead and Barcelona. He was also now becoming known as a Christian. Requests to speak were pouring in, as they still do, and he had to be very careful not to overcommit himself. The four preoccupations of his life did not always harmonise easily – his army job, his athletics, his Christian speaking engagements and his family. He felt pulled in different directions on occasions. It helped a little that the Christians in Sport office began to act as a clearing house for all his speaking engagements.

The Commonwealth Games came and went, and Kriss collected his gold medal for the individual event. Another would surely have come his way but for a hotly disputed disqualification in the 4×400 metres relay. This incident, which involved a baton change, left a bad taste in the mouth and provoked an angry protest from the English 4×100 metres team led by Linford Christie.

The Christian fellowship in the team continued with regular meetings in the Village. They were not quite the blockbusters of Seoul, but it was a time of consolidation and development. What became clear to Kriss and his friends, and indeed to me as a chaplain, was that there was a need for somebody to be available regularly on the track and field scene to pastor athletes and organise meetings. Soon afterwards such a person was found in Mark McAllister, a recent graduate from London Bible College, and a competent middle distance runner himself.

So when the team set off for Split and the European Championships, Mark went too. By now Richard Nerurker, also a Christian, had emerged in the team to run 10,000 metres. Sadly neither Edwards nor Samuels, though selected for the triple jump, had managed the qualifying distance. Each day there were meetings in hotel rooms to encourage individuals and Mark was always at the trackside cheering. The Great Britain coach, Frank Dick, with whom it has to be said Akabusi had not always enjoyed the warmest relationship, totally backed the athletes' request for a chaplain and did his utmost to smooth the way. Mark discovered that he had an important role to play with many in the team regardless of their faith or lack of it. Several sought him out for a chat when they got used to seeing his face around.

Of course, the European Championship was the place where Akabusi's greatest dream became a reality – he broke David Hemery's record of 48.12. "I must admit," he says, "that my victory in Split was the most emotional moment of my athletics career. I know I went loopy but there was a relief at having won, which was expected, as that was my whole intention of going to the Championships. On my way to the stadium I told Roger Black, 'I'm going to run 47.95 today.' It was almost half a minute after the finish that I saw my time (47.92) and I thought someone must be stitching me up – it had to be a joke. However, when the full realisation of what I had run hit me, all I wanted to do was rush around and tell somebody and then it was after this 'loopy period' that I settled down and said, 'Thank you, Lord.'"

There was also a big televised kiss from Monika, and seemingly endless television interviews. In all of them Kriss was exhuberant, laughing, modest and very proud. He never failed to acknowledge God's activity in his life and provided a splendid role model of Christian manliness for the millions watching. It was a very special moment in British athletics. The race itself had gone according to plan. He made a controlled, almost cautious start – "I wanted to clear the first five hurdles cleanly without any mistake in 13 strides and I did just that." From number five on it was a flat out charge. Whittingham's coaching paid off – with the accelerator full down he controlled his technique better than he had ever done before. After hurdle seven he changed to 14 strides, and after nine came home in 15. "Changing down costs time" says Whittingham, "so Kriss thinks he can go at least 0.5 seconds faster in future." So "playing safe" by changing the number of strides secured victory and gives hope of even greater things to come.

The European Championships were a great triumph for Frank Dick and the British team. Gold medals for Yvonne Murray, Colin Jackson, Steven Backley, John Regis, Linford Christie, Roger Black, Tom McKean and Kriss were capped by an epic 4×400 metre relay, with Regis coming in at the last minute. Sanders gave the team a steady start with 45.85, Akabusi was timed at a blistering 44.48 and gave the baton to Regis, the 200 metres gold medallist, who clocked a staggering leg of 43.93, the fastest of the day. Roger Black, the individual gold medallist, coasted home ahead of the field. Black recognised the importance of Kriss's role. "The second and third baton changes were fantastic," he said.

Returning home victorious Akabusi decided the time had come to leave the Army, which had so helped him with athletics, and move on to new things. "The system gave me security, support and an alternative to thinking about track and field all the time. It has also helped me to keep my feet on the ground as one minute you are a track star and the next an ordinary soldier doing his job." He reached the rank of Warrant Officer and drew the following words of praise from Lt General Sir John Learmont: "We are extremely proud of the manner in which you have represented the country and the success you have achieved . . . You leave behind a marvellous example for others to follow."

As Kriss sets his mind to the future those comments say it all.

CAREER SUMMARY

Championship medals
Olympics: 1984, 4×400 Silver
Commonwealth: 1990, 400H Gold; 1986, 4×400 Gold
European: 1986, 4×400 Gold; 1990, 400H Gold, 4×400 Gold
World: 1987, 4×400 Silver

Other honours
European Cup:
    1983 4×400 Gold
    1985 4×400 Bronze
    1989 400H Gold, 4×400 Gold
AAA 400 Champion in 1988
UK 400 Champion in 1984; tied 400H in 1987

Records
European and Commonwealth 4×400
Relay records 1984, 1987 and 1990
UK 400H record 1990

Progression

Year	400	400H
1976	52.4	
1977	49.1	
1978	50.2	
1979	48.7	
1980	48.0	
1981	48.0/48.13	
1982	48.0/48.18	
1983	46.10	
1984	45.43	
1985	45.55	
1986	45.65	
1987	45.99	48.64
1988	44.93	48.67
1989	46.3	48.59
1990	47.1	47.92

Other personal bests
100: 10.7
200: 21.46/ 21.3/ 21.2 (wind assisted)
300: 32.76
800: 1:48.2
110H: 14.6

GARTH CROOKS

When the 14-year-old Garth Crooks watched his beloved Stoke City beat Chelsea 2–1 in the 1972 League Cup Final, to win their first ever trophy, inevitably Garth dreamed about playing at Wembley one day. But not in his wildest dreams could he have anticipated playing at Wembley seven times in 16 months (from May 1981 to August 1982).

During that period Tottenham Hotspur reached the League Cup Final and two FA Cup Finals (both of which were replayed) as well as playing in two Charity Shield Matches. But more of that later.

Growing up in Stoke-on-Trent, the only son – he has four sisters – of West Indian parents, Garth Crooks only ever wanted to be a footballer. Butler Street where he lived was so close to Stoke City's Victoria Ground that the young Garth soon came to know how the game was going by the loudness and direction of the shouts. It was not long before he knew the name of every Stoke City player and longed to be one of them himself.

Religion was an early influence. His parents were God-fearing people. His mother used to read the children Bible stories as she got them ready for bed and sent the children to a church school. While Christianity was not a priority for Garth at this stage, seeds were sown in this period which later came to fruition.

His father was far more interested in cricket than football (although Garth's successes did change that), but fortunately for Garth his uncle loved football and started to take him to the games. He reminisces eagerly about Lawrie Leslie, Denis Viollet, Peter Dobing, Eddie Clamp – "Oh, what a player he was and he did clamp you, too" – and other Stoke players of the 'sixties. He recalls seeing Stanley Matthews play for Stoke in a testimonial game against the great Real Madrid.

At school he excelled at sport much more than in the classroom. He played football for his school, St Peter's Secondary Modern, and then for the county. Sport gave him the attention that he was seeking. The disappointment of not being selected for England at schoolboy level passed when he was signed on by his beloved Stoke City as an apprentice professional. "At that stage all I ever wanted was to play for Stoke City. When it happened I remember thanking God." Looking back Garth says, "I meant what I said but at the time I didn't understand the relationship I had with Him."

He established himself in the Stoke City reserves and turned in some excellent performances. So the day came that he got his chance in the Stoke City first team. It was 10th April, 1976. On the previous day, manager Tony Waddington told him that he would play the next day. Stoke lost 1–0 to Coventry but it was a great day for Garth. Incidentally, it is worth noting that while at the time of writing Stoke City are languishing in the Third Division, the team of 1976 which included Peter Shilton and Alan Hudson finished 12th in Division One.

His first goal for Stoke City was against West Ham United. "It wasn't a classic goal. The ball came across the penalty area and I stuck it in. The first to congratulate me was Jimmy Greenhoff, who said, 'About time, too!' That was a helpful lesson to me that looking nice and neat wasn't enough. It was about scoring goals and winning. This was professional football. I was too filled with romance, satisfied just to be playing for Stoke City."

A less happy memory of Stoke was racial abuse. "I came up against a great deal of racism. As a young lad surrounded by 99 per cent white people – you were always made aware that you were a nigger, a wog. You became used to being the butt of all the jokes. When I played football you had the Alf Garnetts in the crowd bringing it down to the lowest common denominator. When I left Stoke I said Stoke-on-Trent never had anything for me and I was glad to get out of the place. It was a bland remark, borne out of those hurts.

"I remember being aware at one game that half the crowd were chanting my name and wishing me well and at the other end supporters showing such anger and they didn't know me from a bar of soap. I used to come home and wonder what it was all about."

By breaking into the Stoke City team Garth had achieved his first ambition. The next year or two transformed him from the talented lad who enjoyed playing football into a professional footballer.

He played for Stoke City for four seasons. During that period they were relegated to Division Two and then promoted back to Division One again. Throughout this period Garth's striking rate was about a goal every three games. He was top scorer three of the four seasons.

During the 1979–80 season Garth was playing pretty well. He particularly enjoyed scoring two goals against Tottenham. That game, in his words, "showed Spurs a hungry young black player who wanted to do it." During that season he was chosen four times by England at Under-21 level. His debut for England Under-21 against Bulgaria in November 1979 was a particular triumph. England won 5–0 and Crooks scored three.

At the end of that season, Garth Crooks signed for Spurs for £600,000. Even though it meant leaving Stoke, where he had lived all his life, and Stoke City, the club he loved, he had not a moment's hesitation in accepting the move.

Tottenham manager, Keith Burkinshaw, said at the time, "Crooks is a good footballer as well as having a pretty good goal-scoring record and we are hoping for exciting things from him and Archibald."

The season could hardly have started better. He scored on his debut for Spurs, a 2–0 win over Nottingham Forest. He ran on to Hoddle's through pass, side-stepped Peter Shilton and scored. He scored four goals in his first three games. Playing alongside Steve Archibald, he thrived on the service provided by the creative midfield talents of Glenn Hoddle and Ossie Ardiles. In league and cups that season Archibald scored 25 goals and Crooks 22.

With Hoddle and Ardiles hitting pin-point balls into the penalty area Garth's greatest assets were his speed, which enabled him to outpace a defender for the 50–50 ball, and his quicksilver reactions and ball control skills which enabled him to pounce quickly on the loose ball and strike.

The Crystal Palace goalkeeper Paul Barron must have been sick of the sight of Garth Crooks that season. In the league Spurs beat Palace home and away with Crooks netting five times. For good measure Spurs also knocked Palace out of the League cup . . . and guess who scored.

Despite all the excitement Spurs drew and lost too many games to mount a serious challenge for the League title. It was a season in which they would win three games in a row and then not win any of the next six, then put together two or three wins then a sequence of draws and defeats. In the FA Cup, however, it all came right.

In the semi-final Spurs drew with Wolves but won the replay 3–0 with Crooks scoring twice from Hoddle's defence-splitting passes. In the Cup Final they met Manchester City. It is the cup final remembered for Tommy Hutchinson of Manchester City scoring at both ends. He put Manchester City ahead in the first half and then had the misfortune to deflect Glenn Hoddle's free-kick into his own goal. The replay, which Spurs won 3–2, is remembered for Ricky Villa's brilliant goal after taking the ball past several defenders. Garth Crooks scored what he calls the "forgotten goal" of the replay. "Everybody remembers the deflection by Tommy Hutchinson and the two goals by Ricky Villa in the replay but everyone forgets my goal. It was a vital goal at the time, though."

So in his first season with Spurs he had scored 22 goals and had a Cup Winner's medal. The transition to the big-time had happened easily. Garth adds the following interesting assessment: "While I was very successful on the field, I lost myself off it. I got carried away with it and spent too much time with those people who want to pat you on the back, rather than the people – like the coaches and manager – who formed the basis of that success."

The 1981–82 season was one which promised a great deal for Tottenham. As the season reached its climax, Spurs were still in with a chance of four trophies – the League title, the League Cup, the FA Cup and the European Cup Winners' Cup.

The first to be decided was the League Cup. Spurs met Liverpool in the final on 13th March. Everything was going well. Spurs led 1–0 with just three minutes to go. Then Ronnie Whelan scored with a shot from 20 yards to take the game into extra time. Liverpool scored twice in extra time to take the trophy 3–1. Losing is bad enough but to lose after being three minutes from victory was hard to bear.

The challenge for the League championship evaporated over the last few weeks of the season, mainly because of fixture congestion – the price of success in the cup competitions – and injuries to key players. In the end they finished fourth, the closest Garth has come to winning the championship. Perhaps with fewer cup games it might have been different, but with Liverpool finishing the season with 13 wins and three draws in their last 16 games, they would have taken some stopping.

They reached the FA Cup Final again that year against Queen's Park Rangers. In a repeat of the previous year, the final ended 1–1 with Spurs winning 1–0 in the replay.

Their successes in domestic football got Spurs into Europe. This proved to be a real highlight of Garth's career. Spurs played in European competition in four of Garth's five seasons with the club. He recalls, "The first division is a great place to play but playing in Europe is a bit special, particularly in the later stages of the competition when you come up against some of the world's greatest players. Pitting your wits and talents against the best players in Europe is an exciting challenge. There is a magic that you don't get in a domestic game or even an FA Cup Final."

In 1981–82 in the European Cup Winner's Cup Spurs beat Dundalk (with Crooks scoring twice), Eintracht Frankfurt and Ajax of Amsterdam before facing Barcelona in the semi-final. The second leg in Barcelona was played before 90,000 people with Spurs going out 2–1 on aggregate. In 1983–84 Spurs won the UEFA Cup, beating Anderlecht in the final 4–3 on penalties, after both legs had finished 1–1. Garth did not play in the final but was proud to be part of the Tottenham squad which had won the trophy.

The following year Spurs lost in the quarter-final of the UEFA cup. Two particular memories for Garth were scoring three goals on the night Spurs beat Sporting

Braga 6–0 at White Hart Lane, and playing against Real Madrid in the Bernabeu Stadium in front of 95,000 people. Spurs drew 0–0 but lost the home leg 1–0.

Garth Crooks is without doubt one of the best players never to get a full international cap for England. Garth agrees! "Looking back it was surprising that I never got picked for England. I remember scoring three goals for England Under-21 but Gary Birtles was picked for the next England game. The nearest I came to it was probably the 1982 World Cup when I was picked as a reserve for the party. Kevin Keegan was injured and doubtful for the World Cup. In the end he went but wasn't really fit. If he hadn't gone, perhaps I would have gone instead."

With the benefit of hindsight he adds, "While I would love to have played for England, looking back, if I had played international football, I am not sure that I would have become a Christian when I did. What I mean is, that at that stage of my life I used to find that I couldn't really listen to people or God if there were too many exciting things going on around me. If I had played for England the situation in my life might well have got worse before it got better."

In 1984 there was a brief interlude in the Tottenham period. At the time Spurs had an abundance of quality strikers. Garth found himself in competition with the likes of Steve Archibald, Alan Brazil and Mark Falco for at most two places in the team. As a result he was in and out of the team and playing quite a bit of reserve football.

An approach from Manchester United manager Ron Atkinson led to Garth going on loan to United for two months. He played seven matches in the famous red shirt, scoring two goals. United were second in the League throughout the period he was there. This was a fun period for Garth. He enjoyed being part of Manchester United. He appreciated playing in front of Arnold Muhren, Brian Robson, Ray Wilkins and alongside Frank Stapleton. While the loan did not lead to a transfer, it helped re-establish his career at Tottenham.

The following season, 1984–85, proved to be his last with Tottenham. When Spurs beat Liverpool 1–0 at Anfield, the first time they had beaten Liverpool away from home for 73 years, it was Garth who scored the goal. Nonetheless it was a season in which competition for places was fierce, and despite scoring 10 goals in 22 league games he was in and out of the team.

At the end of the year his contract was up. Spurs offered him a one-year contract. He felt he deserved a longer one. West Bromwich Albion made an offer to buy him. After some thought he decided to leave Tottenham. He describes signing for West Brom as "the one time I have sacrificed my feelings for money. West Brom offered me the moon. I remember driving to West Brom the first time after I signed. By the time I reached Watford I was beginning to wonder if it had all been a big mistake. I ended up signing because of having lots and lots of money put in front of me and hating every minute of it."

West Brom lost nine of their first ten games in 1985–86 and remained bottom of the First Division throughout the season. With five goals in nineteen games Garth was second top scorer. The following season he was top scorer with 11 goals in 21 games – including two against Stoke City – before signing for Charlton Athletic. West Brom finished the season in the middle of Division Two.

During the two years spent at West Brom, he continued to live in London. This was mainly because of property prices. He was reluctant to give up his London property, preferring to commute daily between Birmingham and London. Getting up at about 6.00am to drive to Birmingham required a lot of commitment.

It was the price of continuing to live in London.

He sees this time as a turning point in his life. He recalls: "I used to have these wonderful conversations with God. Actually they weren't conversations – they were monologues. I used to tell Him exactly how I felt, exactly how He had let me down. I had always been taught 'The Lord giveth and the Lord taketh away', but did it have to be so instant? Over a period of 12 months I gave Him the best spiritual lectures imaginable – it might sound whacky but it was vivid at times – with God. I would tell Him, 'It's your fault.'

"This happened for about six months and then I felt God say, 'When you are ready to listen to what I've got to say, you'll shut up and I'll begin to talk but I won't say anything until you have finished! He started to tell me that all the time I was going off and doing my thing He allowed me to do it. He allowed me to go ahead and find out what life is all about. He then said, 'If you had asked me at the time I would have told you at the time. I can't remember you ever asking me what my thoughts were or did I approve of this.' Now when I did, He told me."

Garth realised that he had to sort out his relationship with God. Through the influence of friends like rock singer David Grant he started attending the Kensington Temple, an international charismatic church in Notting Hill.

He recalls vividly his first visit to the church. "I came in and looked around. There were black, brown, yellow, white people. I was impressed with their enthusiasm and commitment. They seemed to put as much into the worship as I put into football. There was great team spirit. They were all very much committed to Jesus Christ. I just felt at home from the moment I came into the church. Then this little fat man stood up. I thought, 'He can't be the preacher.' But he was, and what a preacher. That was my first meeting with

Pastor Wynne Lewis, the senior pastor of Kensington Temple.''

The sermon really challenged him. ''I felt reduced from the celebrity footballer that I thought I was to something quite insignificant in comparison with the Almighty. I just sat there and said, 'I'm sorry. I'm sorry.' I felt God reply, 'Know that I am God.' Up to that point in my life I had looked on God as a friend, as one of the chaps. Suddenly I realised who I was dealing with.''

In March 1987 his exile in Birmingham ended. He was transferred from West Brom to Charlton Athletic. When he signed, Charlton were 20th (third from bottom) in the First Division and looking doomed to relegation. Garth played in the last five games, scoring twice. Charlton won three and drew on the last five – Garth scored the winner in the last game. They finished fourth from bottom and were in the play-off for the last place in Division One with three Second Division teams.

Charlton retained their first division status, but only after a fight. In the play-off semi-final they beat Ipswich and then defeated Leeds United in a marathon final. The two-leg tie finished 2–2. A third match finished 0–0 but in extra time Charlton got the goals that won the game. Seven Wembley appearances with Tottenham were nothing compared with the tension as Charlton battled for their First Division lives.

First-Division survival has become an annual battle for Charlton Athletic. In 1987–88 they finished 17th avoiding the relegation play-offs on goal difference. Garth again played his part as top scorer with 10 of Charlton's 38 league goals. The following year they were 14th but in 1989–90 with Garth injured all season they were finally relegated to Division Two.

Garth Crooks had become involved in the Professional Footballers' Association in 1982 as a member of the management committee. The PFA, founded in 1907, exists to represent the interests of professional footballers. Its role includes helping players through the crises that they face – injury, the end of their career, etc. The PFA runs an Education Fund, a Benevolent Fund and an Accident Insurance Fund to give players help when it is needed. Another important task of the PFA is to make players aware of their responsibility to maintain the good image of football.

In November 1988 the association needed to elect a new chairman to succeed Brian Talbot, and Garth was appointed. He was delighted by his appointment, honoured that his fellow professionals should express their confidence in him in this way. He saw it also as another sign of the recognition given to black players in the game.

The period of his chairmanship proved to be one of unusually high profile for the PFA. Mrs Thatcher's government was intent on passing through Parliament a bill to make identity cards compulsory for all football supporters. The PFA, like all the responsible football bodies, opposed the scheme. Garth found himself in great demand to represent the players' position at meetings, in TV interviews, and so on.

One day a training session at Charlton was interrupted by the Charlton secretary running across the pitch. She spoke to manager Lennie Lawrence who then called Garth over: "Parliament is discussing the Football ID Scheme and they want you to be present." Lennie and Garth exchanged slightly incredulous looks. The idea of a footballer being required at the House of Commons was outside their experience but he had to go. During this period he was conscious "of the danger of being engulfed in the glamour of it all. I asked God constantly to remind me that He was with me".

The 1989–90 season did not exist for Garth. He suffered from a damaged nerve in his back, which meant that he did not play in a single League game. It was a difficult injury to cope with in several ways. He had no broken bone to show and at times people would not believe that he really was injured. It was also unlike any other injury that he had ever experienced. It was out of his hands. There was nothing he could do but wait. I asked him how he had coped with the injury. His answer was: "With great difficulty."

It was a bad year for Lennie Lawrence. Not only were Charlton facing relegation but the greyhound that he owned as a kind of hobby brought him no pleasure either. At one stage he told the press in exasperation that the greyhound was injured "even more often than Garth Crooks"!

In the end he had surgery on his back. Afterwards the surgeon said it was touch and go whether he would ever play football again. He regained fitness, often playing through incredible pain, but by November of the following season it was obvious to him that his back would not stand the pressure of playing professional football.

Looking back, he sees the way it all happened as helpful. "It was as if I was being gradually weaned off a drug. I needed things to fill my time. I got involved in journalism and radio and TV work – a programme on London's Capital Radio, the BBC TV World Cup Panel, a chat show on BBC Radio 5, etc. Suddenly playing football was no longer paramount. When I had to make the decision to give up playing, it was much easier to do."

As a well-paid professional footballer, Garth Crooks lived life to the full. He drove a fast car, was to be seen in the fashionable restaurants and clubs. He led the kind of life people would expect of a footballer. He had a playboy image. At the time he started going regularly to Kensington Temple, his girl-friend was a successful model. He began to see that the relationship was in conflict with what he knew to be the truth. He felt God telling him to break off that relationship. He did so and at the same time asked God for a new Christian girl-friend.

After about six weeks he spotted a rather gorgeous girl sitting opposite him at Kensington Temple. He later discovered that her name was Funkazi. He recalls his first impression: "She was always dressed immaculately. I used to pray just for a chance to meet her. Sometimes I would go to the Wednesday night service just in the hope that she would be there!

"Then Jumoke Fashola, a singer who is a member of KT, invited me to her birthday party. It was 16th January 1987 – I am hopeless at dates but I always remember that one. We played Nottingham Forest away. Jumoke said that it would only be a small group at the party including her flat-mate. I asked who her flat-mate was. She pointed to Funkazi! I couldn't believe it."

He finally managed to speak to her at the end of the party when she was washing the dishes. Strange as it may seem, he says, "After she spoke a few words to me, I knew that she was going to be my wife." The relationship blossomed and being a romantic, Garth wanted to get engaged in Maximes in Paris. "So we went off to Paris for a weekend and went to Maximes on the Saturday night. I proposed to her. She made me get down on one knee. I thought – I've come this far, I'm not going to be beaten now!"

She accepted his proposal but if Garth thought he was home and dry, he was to be sadly disappointed. Funkazi explained that her Nigerian background required him to fulfil certain duties. "The first thing I had to do was to go and speak to her father, who is a Nigerian ambassador.

So off I went to Nigeria. He turned me down." All Funkazi's sisters and other friends at Kensington Temple prayed that he would change his mind. Now Garth had to go off to her village, Orura, in River State, Nigeria, to seek permission from her uncles, brothers and the whole village.

"I flew to Lagos, then four hours by road and finally 30 minutes by speedboat. I remember thinking in the boat, 'What on earth am I doing here?' The whole village came out to hear me. I can tell you, addressing the PFA dinner is nothing after this! They said 'yes' and it was back on the boat."

Garth and Funkazi were married in July 1990 in Cotounu, Republic of Benin in West Africa.

The boy from quite a humble background in Stoke-on-Trent certainly made good. He played alongside some of the greatest players in the world and even had the thrill of scoring at Wembley. He had the honour of being chairman of the Professional Footballers' Association. Now all that is in the past, he could easily be in some kind of crisis. Yet as you speak to him you sense that he knows that his future is in the hands of the same Lord Jesus Christ who has been with him in the good times and the difficult times in his football career.

CAREER SUMMARY

League appearances

Stoke City	1976–80	147	(48 goals)
Tottenham Hotspur	1980–85	125	(48 goals)
Manchester United	1983–84	7	(2 goals)
West Brom	1985–87	40	(16 goals)
Charlton Athletic	1987–90	56	(15 goals)
Total		375	(129 goals)

Transfers

July 1980   Stoke City to Tottenham Hotspur – £600,000
November 1983 to January 1984 Tottenham Hotspur to
   Manchester United – Loan
July 1985   Tottenham Hotspur to West Brom – £100,000
March 1987   West Brom to Charlton Athletic – £75,000

International appearances
4 England Under-21 caps 1980 (3 goals)

Honours
1978–79 Promotion Division 3 to Division 2
1981   FA Cup Winners Medal
1982   FA Cup Winners Medal
         League Cup Runners-Up
1984   UEFA Cup Winners

Other
Chairman of Professional Footballers' Association 1988–1990

GRAHAM, ADRIAN AND LLOYD DAVIES

On 24th February, 1966, the first of three boys was born to Michael and Dorita Davies of Coychurch in South Wales. All three grew up to be fine rugby players and musicians.

There is nothing unusual about that. Wales is full of people called Davies and many of them either play or follow rugby. And music runs in the blood of most true Welshmen. But these three are distinguished by the excellence of their gifts and also by their shared and very sincere Christian faith. The eldest boy was named Graham, Adrian arrived three years later and Lloyd a year after that.

In many ways the Davies are a typical "chapel" family. Michael and Dorita met at Carmel Baptist Church in Llanharran, the church they still attend. Dorita's father was a shopkeeper in the village and Michael's father worked on the railways. They lived in nearby Llanharry. In due course Dorita went to university and got a degree in history and music. Michael qualified as a quantity surveyor through a correspondence course. The boys have inherited not only their parents' talents but also their drive and determination. All three are involved in similar professions to their father.

The chapel dominated the family's lives. Its ever present influence culminated in enforced attendance on Sundays. Graham feels that his parents' attitudes mellowed somewhat as the younger boys grew up.

Where he was concerned there was no thought of participating in organised sport on a Sunday, whereas Adrian and Lloyd were permitted to play in the occasional mini-rugby tournament.

Times were changing rapidly, of course. The turbulent social revolution of the 'sixties was in full swing, though perhaps it took longer to reach South Wales than most places. The economic stability of the region was also under attack as the traditional mining and steel industries fell into decline. Rugby and music provided the unchangeable background to the fabric of Welsh society. The 'seventies, as the Davies boys began to take an interest, were glory years for Welsh rugby. The Pontypool front row, Price, Faulkner and Winsor, provided the platform in the scrum for a dashing back row comprising the likes of Terry Cobner, Mervyn Davies and John Taylor, and then there were those unforgettable backs.

Every Saturday of the international season, it seemed, you could hear Cliff Morgan or Bill McLaren on the television: "Edwards to John, John to Dawes, Dawes to Gravell, Gravell to Gerald Davies . . . Davies is tackled, slips it to J. P. R. Williams . . . What a try!" And then when Barry John retired along came Phil Bennett and the magic went on. Wales swept all before them in that era and the fervour ran high down in Coychurch.

But the Christian lifestyle and standards of the family meant that sport rarely became the totally dominant force that it does in some families. Graham looks back with gratitude to those firm foundations on which he has been able to build his own life and faith. He is very aware of the difficulties that many in rugby have of making the connection between sport and Christianity. They think that God cannot possibly have any interest in the supposedly macho world of top level sport. Graham,

Adrian and Lloyd are living examples of how wrong this attitude is. An awareness of God and a basic belief in Christianity were instilled into them at a very early age. As Graham looks back he recalls that they all knew a great deal about God as teenagers but did not know Him personally. But at least they had the information on which to base a decision of their own. As each has thought through the direction of his life and his priorities, he has come to trust in the basic truth of Christianity and has grown in his personal relationship with God.

They all attended the primary school at Llanharran until they were 11. There Elwyn Jenkins, a fanatical rugby man, communicated a love of the game to the boys. Their father, in fact, had been a soccer player representing Wales at youth level, but it was rugby that captured the attention of his sons.

As youngsters they played for East Wales at under-eleven level. Neither Graham nor Lloyd played in the "big" match against West Wales, both being "substitutes". But Adrian, who is without question the most talented of the three brothers, captained the team in his year. It was his first match at Cardiff Arms Park and the main family memory appears to be that he missed a conversion from right under the posts! They all progressed to the relevant youth teams. Lloyd became a full-back, Adrian a fly-half (although he was to win his first cap for Wales in the centre) and Graham a left-winger.

Adrian combined his rugby with excellence in cricket and soccer, representing Wales at schoolboy level at all three. In fact, when he was in the Under-15 group he preferred soccer to rugby. He toured Europe with the team and gave serious consideration to a career in professional football.

At Pencoed Comprehensive School they all revealed

remarkable depth and variety of talent as schoolboys. Apart from sport at which, of course, they excelled, they all became proficient pianists, and can play a number of other instruments as well. They also revealed considerable academic ability. Speaking very honestly and movingly to an audience of 600 fellow students in Cambridge just before the 1990 Varsity match, Adrian explained, quite without boasting, how he came to terms with the extraordinary talents he possesses. "I realised," he said, "that God had given me great gifts; that I was able to do most things I wanted to. I couldn't just ignore the Person who had given me these things."

Graham's wife Kathy laughs at this story: "Typical, and he's good looking!"

As teenagers they played and worked hard. It was not unusual to play football and rugby on the same day, and then be involved in a concert in the evening. Nor did they neglect their studies. In due course Graham secured a place at the University of Wales Institute of Science and Technology (UWIST) to read Architecture. Adrian headed for Cambridge to read Geography, and Lloyd to the University of Wales in Cardiff to study Town Planning. After a while Adrian transferred to Land Economy, a course much favoured by Cambridge sportsmen!

Each of them found sport, music and academic studies quite enough to occupy their minds. Graham recalls telling Adrian one Sunday morning that whatever happened he would not go to chapel when he grew up. Then when Graham was in the lower sixth form at school a close friend, Susan, was killed in a car crash. It was the first time any of them had encountered death. Graham, who helped carry the coffin at the funeral, found himself thinking seriously about death and about God. The dead girl had been an integral part of the chapel community, and the Davieses experienced God's comfort and love in what was a very sad time for the fellowship.

But that experience was soon crowded out by the distractions of sixth form life, which revolved around rugby and the orchestra and the girl-friends that were associated with each activity. In the Welsh Schools XV Graham began to experiment with the faster side of life as he saw it. "It wasn't a great success," he recalls. "A belly full of ale left me feeling not only ill, but guilty as well. My life at that time lacked an essential ingredient, but I did not know what it was and so the wine, women and song continued."

On the last Sunday before he set of for UWIST Graham decided to go to chapel. As much as anything it was to say goodbye to lots of people who were very special to him. Perhaps he was vulnerable as he prepared to leave home, perhaps God had prepared his heart through the experience of Susan's death – we cannot know. But Graham and Adrian heard the Good News about Jesus in a totally new way that evening.

At the end of the service the minister invited those who wanted to give their lives to the Lord to come forward. Graham knew he wanted to change. Earlier in the service there had been a baptism, and as he watched the lady coming up out of the water Graham detected a real change in her. Being very self-conscious like most teenagers, he was embarrassed about going forward. But he found he could no longer stay sitting in his seat and somehow stumbled to the front. Perhaps influenced by his older brother's initiative, Adrian also went forward.

They see it as the time they "saw the light". It was a surprise to everyone else in church. According to Graham they were "gob-smacked". The assumption had been that the Davies brothers were Christians – after all, their parents were leading members of the chapel. They had attended all their lives, they were nice, clean-living, decent and respectable lads. What was going on?

The boys were doing what many people miss out on. They were turning an inherited faith into a personal faith. Both look back on that Sunday as a crucial time. The assumption that they were Christians, just because their parents were and because they grew up in the chapel, no longer held water. As they heard the Bible explained, learning that God longed for a personal response from them and that He deserved such a response because He had sent His only Son, Jesus Christ, to die for them, they decided that following that same living Jesus was the way for them.

Adrian continued at school for another two years and Lloyd for another three. They both distinguished themselves on the sports field. Lloyd got his golf handicap down to eleven and Adrian increasingly became a cause of great speculation in the world of rugby. Everyone remembered the great years of John and Bennett. Jonathan Davies promised great things but "went North", signing a professional contact with Rugby League club, Widnes. Could it be that Adrian Davies would assume the most coveted and the most pressured position in Welsh sport – fly-half for the national team?

At UWIST Graham discovered that "being" a Christian, as opposed to "becoming" one, was not at all easy. "For twelve months," he says, "I lost the battle." The situation was made worse by a serious knee ligament injury which put him out of rugby for a year from November 1984. He was pretty desperate during that first term at college. Everything had gone more or less as planned in his life until then. Suddenly he faced a serious threat to his sporting ambitions, and he found that his faith constantly nagged at him if he joined in with the more drunken exploits of his rugby-playing friends.

He was in the tension in which many in sport find themselves: torn between their personal desire to follow Christ and His teaching and the temptation to compromise and join in with "the gang". The apostle Paul writing to a small group of Christian people in Rome 2,000 years ago experienced the same tension: "What I want to do I do not do, but what I hate I do . . . I have the desire to do good but I cannot carry it out" (Romans 6:15–18). In that passage in the Bible Paul cries out, "Who will rescue me?"

God rescued Graham in the attractive person of the girl who was to become his wife! Kathy was a strong Christian who was very involved in the Christian Union. One day towards the end of that first year at college she knocked on Graham's door. She was, in fact, ignoring the advice of two people who have since become very special friends. They had told her to watch out for the dubious character who played rugby. The only time Graham had been to the Christian Union was to a meeting at the beginning of the year when free food was on offer, but he was not about to turn Kathy's invitation down and so he became involved with a group of young, vibrant, contemporary Christians.

The whole Christian scene at college was a new experience for him. He was used to the old authorised version of the Bible, nineteenth-century hymns and a formal service on Sundays. Now he discovered modern translations of the Scriptures, songs that could be accompanied by guitars, and freedom in worship. He loved every minute of it and has never looked back.

During the 1985–86 rugby season, his first full season with Neath, he put his sport and his faith together. The season culminated with a tour to Italy by the Wales B squad. Graham was thrilled to be selected and played in four matches including the "Test". The game played at the Olympic stadium in Rome was drawn 9–9 and Graham suffered a severe ankle injury in the second half which necessitated leaving the field. Nevertheless, he felt he played well and that full international honours would not be long in coming.

Even more importantly, he felt that he took a positive stand as a Christian on a rugby tour for the first time. He remembers assembling with the squad and thinking, "Oh no, what a motley crew!" He was frightened of how they would react to the college boy Christian. To his amazement, and as team spirit developed, he found that the firmer the stand he took as a Christian, the more respect he earned. Several of the players came to speak to him privately about their problems or about his faith. He was very encouraged. He began to see that his talent at rugby was not an accident, nor indeed just something which enriched his own life. It was a sacred gift from God that gave him wonderful opportunities to live boldly for God and shine as a light in the rugby world.

That summer Graham joined a team of hundreds of young people who travelled with the Christian organisation, Youth With A Mission, to Edinburgh for the Commonwealth Games. They all slept on the floors of church halls and got involved in witnessing to the thousands of visitors in Edinburgh.

He won two more Welsh "B" caps – both were against France. Wales won at Pontypridd in the 86–87 season and lost a year later at Bourdeaux. He also won a Wales Under-21 cap against Scotland at Wrexham. Graham regrets that he has not yet scored a try in a Welsh jersey.

During the 87–88 season Graham and Adrian found themselves playing together at Neath. The high point was the Cup Final against Llanelli at Cardiff Arms Park which Neath lost despite Adrian's try. Both youngsters got a real buzz from playing in front of 50,000 people. It was a game dominated by the brilliance of Jonathan Davies and only went to emphasise the loss he has been to Welsh Rugby Union since turning professional.

During that summer Adrian worked on a building site. He struggled with his faith at this time. Graham would come home from college full of the joy of being a Christian, whereas for Adrian it seemed like he had to express his faith by saying "no" to quite a lot of things he would have liked to do. He was voted the Most Promising Player of the Year by the Sports Writers' Association – a highly prestigious award.

All the boys faced great changes in October 1988. Lloyd began his Town Planning course at Cardiff, Adrian went up to Robinson College, Cambridge, and Graham to Magdalene College at the same university.

Graham and Adrian left behind secure places in one of the strongest club sides in the country in order to play student rugby. Many in Wales would think of such a move as a step backwards in any attempt to gain international recognition. The next few seasons they played almost all their rugby away from the Welsh limelight. Despite the reduced exposure, neither regrets his decision – in fact Lloyd intends to follow in their footsteps when he has completed his studies at Cardiff where he plays full-back for the University team.

Graham and Adrian feel that the challenge of Cambridge rugby actually improved their skills. Every time they played against first class opposition they knew they had to be at their very best to make up for the lack of experience and, in the forwards, sheer physical size. As two of the better players in the team they had great responsibility – there could be no resting on their laurels or relying on others to get them out of trouble. Graham, in fact, played 51 games for Cambridge in two years. His game expanded during this time and he developed as a thinking tactical left-winger. He reckons he reads the game well, and is good in defence. Without being a brilliant tackler (he is by no means a big man) he works the angles well and causes his opponents to run out of space. His handling is good.

He returned to Cardiff towards the end of the 1989–90 season and made the left-wing position his own as Neath swept all before them, winning the Western Mail Championship, the Whitbread Table and the Schweppes Cup for a unique and never-to-be-repeated treble. In 1990–91 Neath dominated the newly-formed Heineken League.

He's been unlucky that twice he has been seen to drop scoring passes in the full blaze of television cameras. The first was in the 1989 Varsity match, and the second playing for Neath against Bridgend in 1990. It irritates him that the great Phil Bennett was heard to say in his commentary, "Not a very good effort that by the winger." It is an example of how an incident, trivial in itself, can haunt a top sportsperson's life. Graham was playing out of position on the right wing against Bridgend and the angles were unfamiliar. All the difficult passes he has caught seem to be forgotten when one public error occurs.

It can be tough for a young person thrust into the headlines. Adrian recalls travelling home from Newport where Neath had played Cardiff in the semi-final in the Cup in 1988. He was in the train with David Evans, the Oxford and Cardiff centre/fly-half when a group of Neath supporters came past. They recognised the international Evans and not Adrian. Much to Evans' amusement, and with his encouragement, they laid into Adrian verbally, rubbishing him for all they were worth. As they got off the train Evans stopped them and said, "Excuse me, lads, I'd just like to introduce you to my friend here – he's Adrian Davies!"

This kind of incident, or the rather more serious comments of the Press, can hurt. Graham shrugs his shoulders: "It is something you have to learn to live with – mind you, it is easier with God's help."

Adrian has developed into a fine all-round fly-half. Often he controls the game from that key pivotal position. He kicks well with both feet, runs well with a good sidestep and is surprisingly durable for quite a slight man. Graham feels that his bravery, his ability to take a tackle, will be a vital factor as he progresses in international rugby.

Oxford and Cambridge rugby arouses immense passion from its supporters and a deafening lack of interest from everyone else. Adrian and Graham's careers coincided with renewed interest in the annual December Varsity match at Twickenham. It is a unique occasion for all those who play. The players reach a level of fitness which they may never attain again and play with a passion and commitment which is second to none. A feature in every game is the ferocious tackling which sometimes inevitably produces a scrappy game because it leads to errors from the ball carrier. The England fly-half Rob Andrew has said that playing for Cambridge against Oxford at Twickenham was more nerve-racking and more exciting than winning his first cap for England. Perhaps it is the history of it, perhaps it is just that so much seems to hang on the result of just one game. But it is a great occasion in any rugby player's life.

Over 50,000 packed into the stadium in 1988 to watch the Australian Brian Smith mastermind an Oxford victory. In 1989 the boot was on the other foot as Adrian Davies orchestrated a Cambridge victory. Cambridge began sensationally with Graham scoring in the left-hand corner, but an Oxford rally was snuffed out in the second half by Adrian's reliable kicking and finally his try resulting from an Oxford breakdown and a kick ahead.

On 7th October, 1990, Adrian broke away from preparations for the Cambridge season to join the Welsh squad and prepare for the match against the Barbarians to celebrate the Welsh Rugby Union's centenary. He did not expect to play but in the forty-seventh minute Mark Ring was forced off with injury and Adrian won his first cap. He had a quiet game as the Barbarians won 31 points to 24 but did enough to retain his place in the squad, and the prospect of the World Cup in 1991 gave hope for more caps in the future.

In the 1990 Varsity match Oxford stunned Cambridge with a brilliant forward display. The dark blues ran out winners by 21 points to 12 with Adrian Davies kicking eight of his team's points. The game was played in front of 57,000 spectators – a capacity crowd at Twickenham.

At Cambridge Adrian grew in his Christian faith and commitment. With the support of other Christians in the sports scene, he began to apply his faith more effectively amongst his friends in the rugby team. They respected him enormously as a player, of course, and they enjoyed his musical talent off the field. Gradually they came to see that there was a great deal to the quiet youngster from Wales and many became intrigued enough by his faith to start asking questions.

Rugby has already provided Adrian and Graham with many friends and thrills. They carry their great talents with modesty. They are personally warm and attractive people. They will do well in their chosen careers. But both know that "winning is not enough". Their upbringing, the trauma of losing a teenage friend and the opportunities of studying have all convinced them that by far the most important thing in life is to live lives worthy of God.

They remain passionate Welshmen determined to represent their country and their club on the rugby field as often as they can. There is a great intensity about them which is typical of Welsh rugby players. What they are managing to do, and long may it last, is to combine their passion for sport with their passion for Christ.

CAREER SUMMARIES

Graham Davies

Wales Schools	1983–84
Wales Students	1985–89
Wales (U21)	1986
Wales "B" v Italy "B" (Rome)	1986
v France "B" (Pontypridd)	1986
v France "B" (Bordeaux)	1987
Cambridge Blue	1988
Cambridge Blue	1989
Member of the Neath team which won the Heineken League Premier Division	1991

Tours

Canada Bridgend & District Schools	1981
Italy Wales "B"	1986
Inaugural Students World Cup	1988
Taiwan Cambridge University	1988
Japan Cambridge University	1990

Also represented
Crawshaws XV
Welsh Academicals

+50 games for Cambridge University	1988–90
+100 games for Neath RUFC	1985–present

Adrian

East Wales U11 – Captain	1980
Wales Schools Football U15	
Wales Schools Rugby	1985–86
Wales Schools Rugby – Captain	1986–87
Wales U19 Rugby – Captain	1987
Wales Students	1986–present
Wales "B" v France "B"	1990
Wales v Barbarians	1990
Barbarians	
Crawshays	
Cambridge Blue	'88, '89, '90
Cambridge Blue – Captain	'90, '91

CAREER SUMMARIES

Tours

New Zealand (Captain) Wales U19	1987
Oxbridge – Australia/NZ	1989
Japan Cambridge	1990
Sicily Cambridge	1990
Inaugural Students World Cup	1988

also

Welsh Young Player of the Year	1987
Mid Glamorgan Schools Cricket	U15, 16 & 19

Lloyd

Mid Glamorgan Schools (Rugby) U14, 15, 16 & 19	
Wales Universities	1989, 90–91
Wales Students U20	1989 & 90
Combined British Universities	1991
Vice Captain Univ Wales College Cardiff	1989 & 90
Winners of UAU	1991

Tours

UWCC – Texas	1990

Represented

Mid Glamorgan Schools Cricket	U15, 17, 19

KITRINA DOUGLAS

When Kitrina Douglas won the gold medal for drama at the Bath Festival, the last thing she seemed likely to finish up as was a professional golfer.

As a teenager Kitrina had a range of interests. She was good at most sports, playing hockey, tennis, netball and swimming for her school. She reckons she was probably just under county standard in tennis and badminton. However, she didn't play any one sport enough to realise her full potential.

The introduction to golf came on a family holiday in Scotland in 1977. Her father was having a golf lesson and Kitrina, then aged 17, went along. After her father's lesson, she was invited to hit some shots. She recalls replying, "Do I have to?" She hit a few shots. She impressed her father's coach, Gordon Cosh, the Scottish International player who remarked that it was a pity that Kitrina had not taken up golf earlier as she seemed to have natural ability.

Kitrina's father had played semi-pro football and was a good all-round sportsman. She had inherited his aptitude for sport. That evening, to Kitrina's surprise, her father suggested that she leave school at Christmas and spend a year playing golf to see how good she could become. If it didn't work out, she could go back to her studies the next year.

At the end of the summer holidays, she went back to school and announced that she would be leaving at

Christmas to become a golfer. A teacher remarked, "Oh, are you very good at golf?"

Kitrina replied, "No, I've never played before!"

For the next year she devoted herself to golf, playing and practising every day as well as having regular coaching from a top professional, Gordon Brand senior. The schedule was carefully planned. "My father made up a timetable for every day of the week. Early morning running, then long shots, then putting, lunch, in the afternoon chipping, then bunker shots and then I would play a round. So from day one I was professional in my attitude to diet, fitness, behaviour, practice, etc. So when I became a professional I didn't need to change anything."

Progress in the first year – her handicap dropped from the beginner's 36 to 19 – was sufficient to justify extending one year to two. By the end of the second year her handicap had dropped to 3. Now she was in business.

In 1980 she won the Gloucestershire championship (she retained it in each of the following four years), and in 1981 she won the Scottish Girls' Open Stroke Play.

At the time Kitrina followed the course of action she had decided on without a great deal of soul-searching. On reflection she can see how amazing it all was. "Looking back it is a bit unbelievable. My father's thinking was that I was good at all sports. He had played football but that is a sport where you are finished at 30 and you depend on being picked. Golf takes you all over the world and you can play until you have one foot in the grave and you don't depend on anyone else. So golf had a lot going for it. In any case, if it didn't work out I could go back to my studies."

The real breakthrough came in 1982, when she won the British Amateur title, beating Gillian Stewart in the final. The same year she was selected for the Great Britain team for the biennial Curtis Cup match against the United States in Denver, Colorado. In four years she had gone from beginner to British Champion.

Kitrina approached the British Women's Amateur Championship in June 1982 at Walton Heath, Surrey, convinced that the only way she could be certain of a place in the Curtis Cup team was to win the tournament.

The format of the Championship was that all competitors played two rounds with the top 64 going into a match play (knock-out) stage. Kitrina started badly. An 85 left her 15 shots behind the leader. A 78 on the second day left her 18 shots behind leaders Marta Figueras-Dotti and top seed Marie Laure de Lorenzi de Taya, but she had made it into the top 64, without a shot to spare. That a disappointing 85 proved only to be the spur to do better next day was an early example of the "never say die" attitude which has served her so well in her professional career.

The following day Kitrina safely negotiated the first and second rounds. Two more wins put her in the semi-final. Under the headline "Unexpected intruder", John Hennessy wrote in *The Times*, "Katrina (sic) Douglas who survived the qualifying stage of the British Women's Amateur Golf Championship by only a single stroke, reached the semi-final stage of the match play, a totally unexpected intruder among a group of experienced players."

A win over Mary McKenna in the semi-final at the 19th hole put her in the final against Gillian Stewart. Kitrina was two holes down after five but won the next five holes to go three up. She held the lead to win four and two (four up with two to play). Incidentally *The Times* report again called her Katrina, a misspelling which has often been repeated throughout her golf career.

Kitrina, however, did not share the journalists'

surprise: "Winning the British didn't seem that big a breakthrough for me. I had been making progress and winning tournaments regularly for a few years. The British was just another tournament. I really wanted to get into the Curtis Cup team and I reached the stage that the only way I could make the team was to win the British Championship. So I went to win. I prepared for it the way I would today for the Open. All through the winter, I was working towards the British Championship."

The prize for winning – in addition to the cup and the honour – was selection for the British team in the Curtis Cup. The venue was Denver Country Club, a tranquil setting in the shadow of the Rocky Mountains. The match result was 14½ to 3½ in favour of the Americans. Kitrina, teaming up with Janet Soulsby, played two excellent foursomes against Kathy Baker and Laury Smith, halving one and losing the other by the narrowest of margins. She lost both her singles. The match result had a certain inevitability about it as the US had won the cup on the eleven previous meetings. Nonetheless, for Kitrina it was a great experience just to be part of it.

The family in which Kitrina grew up was a Christian family. When she was seven she was in church with her father. When the preacher asked if anyone wanted to give his or her life to Jesus, Kitrina nudged her father and asked if it was all right to put her hand up. She became a Christian that night.

However, over the next 10 or so years there was not a lot of growth in her Christian life. While she went to church, God was not really Number One in her life. When she played in America and she found herself sharing a room with various players, as she puts it: "I didn't exactly hide my light under a bushel, more under the bedclothes!"

The successes in 1982 – British Champion and Curtis

Cup – were marred by her father's death the same year. This was a devastating blow as the Douglases were a close-knit family. Moreover, in addition to the emotional loss, it had severe practical implications for Kitrina. It was her father who had encouraged her to take up golf in the first place. It was he who supported her financially as she played as an amateur.

The year 1983 was a difficult one for Kitrina. With the loss of her father's support, she found herself doing a string of odd jobs to pay for her golf. In addition, she had already fulfilled her ambitions as an amateur. As Alexander the Great before her, she found there were no more kingdoms to conquer.

Women's Professional Golf effectively got off the ground in 1979. After a slow beginning the sport has developed dramatically. Compare top money-winner Alison Sheard's £4,965 in 1979 with Marie-Laure de Lorenzi's £99,360 in 1988. In the 1990s around £2 million prize money is on offer on a tour which takes in Belgium, France, Germany, Italy, Spain, Sweden and Switzerland as well as the UK.

At the beginning of 1984, Kitrina decided to end her amateur career and apply for membership of the Women's Professional Golf Association. So without any sponsorship and with a sizeable overdraft, the result of a winter's practice in Portugal, Kitrina set off for Woburn to play in the Ford Ladies' Golf Classic.

On the playing side, things could hardly have started better. She won her first tournament. After rounds of 73, 75 and 73, she entered the final round in second place, two shots behind Peggy Conley from USA. She had closed the gap after five holes. With Conley dropping back, Kitrina sealed her victory with a superb 9 iron to six feet from the hole for a birdie 3 and a round of 71 (4 under par) to win by four shots. Kitrina recalls it like this:

"The final round was a high tension affair, played like matchplay, but with the gnawing feeling that someone could overtake us without us knowing. The first on-course scoreboard was at the 15th, and to my relief and thrill K. Douglas was at the top, in bold red, two shots clear of Conley and five clear of our next rival. I could hardly believe it; my first tournament and with three holes to play I was two clear of my playing partner and couldn't be caught by anyone else!

"We both dropped a shot at the 16th, the only loose shot I played all day. I made a very nervous par down 17, but my playing partner bogied. That put me three clear going to the last. I must have been the only person there thinking I could still lose, but a well-hit drive into a perfect position left an easy approach, a 9 iron to six feet left me with a birdie to finish four ahead.

"I knew the sort of feeling I can only describe as like going over a hump-backed bridge, when your stomach goes up in the air. I walked off the course six inches above the ground. We left the club soon after the presentation and when I arrived home all my family – aunts, uncles, cousins, nieces and nephews – were waiting, and we had an impromptu party to celebrate."

Her victory was marred somewhat when a WPGA official came with a message from the committee. "They don't like your trousers and they don't like your shoes" were the words he used. She was deeply hurt.

However, the £3,000 winning cheque enabled her not only to equip herself with new shoes and trousers, but also to pay off her overdraft.

Incidentally, that was not her only brush with petty-minded attitudes from the officials who ran the WPGA in those days. She was also fined £100 for arriving 20 minutes late at a cocktail party before the Jersey Open.

One lesson Kitrina had to learn in the professional

ranks was not to believe everything that was said to her.

When she won her first tournament she began to attract the sponsors. First of all a clothing company took her to lunch and offered her a good contract. Then there was a sausage manufacturer who wanted her to do TV advertisements. Only Minolta cameras – of all who promised – actually came up with the money.

Kitrina did pick up £500 as "Rookie of the Year" in 1984. She also gained the honour of being White Horse Whisky Golf Personality of the month for June 1984 – only the second woman to be selected for the award. However, what do you do with a gallon of whisky if you don't drink the stuff!

An ironic response to the criticism of her clothes was the formation of her own sportswear company, Deluxe Sports. Her sister Karen was already in the rag trade at the time and the company was formed to market a range of golf and other sportswear.

By the end of the 1990 season, Kitrina had added another five victories to the initial win in the 1984 Ford Classic.

The first of these was the Hoganas Swedish Open in 1984, played at Molle. Kitrina, coming into the tournament in great form with top four finishes in the previous seven tournaments, shared the lead with a Swedish player, Anna Oxenstierna, after three rounds. When Kitrina and Anna played together in the final round, Kitrina was soon under pressure as her Swedish opponent, to the delight of the home support, opened with a birdie, par, eagle, to be four shots ahead after three holes. Kitrina was not deterred. By the 9th hole she had cut the lead to one shot and by the 14th she was ahead. In the end Kitrina won by three shots from Liselotte Neumann with Oxenstierna a further shot behind.

In 1985 she finished second three times but did not

record a victory. Then in 1986 she won the Mitsubishi
Colt Cars Jersey Open at the Royal Jersey Club. Kitrina
led after two rounds and held the lead with rounds of 71,
67, 71, 69, to win by six shots from Peggy Conley.

In 1987 Kitrina pulled off by far her best win so far, the
Hennessey Cognac Ladies' Cup at Paris St Germain. She
entered the final round one shot behind Laura Davies.
While Laura's challenge evaporated with an 80, Kitrina
held her game together with a 71 to win by three shots. A
particularly satisfying aspect of her victory was beating
Nancy Lopez, arguably the best ever woman golfer, into
second place. The first prize of £10,500 was the biggest
Kitrina had won. Kitrina's performance so impressed the
French magazine *Golf Europeen* that they referred to her as
"Madame Steady", which is certainly an apt description
of how she plays.

A year without a victory (1988) was compensated for
by the double success of 1989. Against the spectacular
back-drop of the Alps, Kitrina won the St Moritz Ladies'
Classic. It was not a tournament that she really looked
like winning. First Florence Descampe led and then
Suzanne Strudwick. With a late run – three birdies in the
last five holes – Kitrina tied Strudwick to force a play-off.
Kitrina won the first play-off hole to take the title.

Winning the tournament was the perfect end to a
memorable week as Kitrina and another professional had
decided to exchange the hassle of air travel for a journey
to Switzerland on the Orient Express. Kitrina described
the experience in her column in *Executive Golfer*.

"I boarded the train at London Victoria at 11.30am and
disembarked after a beautiful breakfast at Zurich, 6.30am
the following morning, refreshed, contented and ready
to play some golf.

"We saw fields of grass gently swaying in the breeze,
we watched barges chugging down the canals with

picnickers lining the banks; we travelled through plains, hills and mountains as the gentle rocking motion lulled us through a time warp to a once forgotten age of the genteel traveller, on her way to Switzerland.

"A pianist playing, attention to detail; Champagne and Hors d'Oeuvres were followed by a light three-course lunch, a short ferry crossing and then back to luxury."

Kitrina also won the Godiva European Master's in Brussels in September 1989. She started the final round level with the French player Marie-Laure de Lorenzi, her playing partner. Both shot 70 to tie for first place. For the second time that summer Kitrina found herself in a play-off and for the second time a successful one. That the European Master's title was second only in prestige to the British Open was shown by the £16,500 first prize.

The one major tournament in Europe which has so far eluded Kitrina is the British Open, the most prestigious on the European calendar. She has come close to winning on a number of occasions. In 1988 at Lindrick she shared the half-way lead with Corrinne Dibnah, the eventual winner, before finishing sixth.

In 1989 she finished eighth, the top British player. In 1990 at Woburn during a heat-wave she had a real go at it. However, the week could have started better as she was stung by a wasp while practising.

She led the tournament at the half-way stage playing inspired golf only to be overtaken on the final day by Helen Alfredsson and Jane Hill. At one stage in the second round Kitrina had been nine under par for the tournament compared to the winning score of four under.

When I suggested to her that it must be disappointing not to have won after playing so well, she replied that playing well and winning are not the same thing and that she had played well most of the season but not won.

The life of the professional golfer is not as glamorous in reality as it may appear. Golf tournaments last four days, but are usually preceded by a Pro-Am. Most players like a day to practise. As a result the pattern tends to be six days away and one at home with players travelling to tournaments all over Europe. They fly or drive – or travel on the Orient Express – as suits them.

It may be fun once, but when you do it for the twentieth time in the season it can become tedious. Kitrina admits to having the same kind of Monday morning feelings that anyone else might have. I remember once asking her if she had had a good time in France where she had been playing in a tournament. Kitrina's reply was to ask if I had had a good time in the office that week! It was a timely reminder that golf for her is not so much a game as a job of work. As Kitrina says, "I treat golf as a profession. It's like going to the office. I take my lunch break and then I return to work."

Travelling is not without its moments of drama. Early in her career, Kitrina drove to Paris and parked outside the house of the Christian family with whom she was staying. On the first night someone broke into the car and stole tapes and other items. On the second night the car was stolen!

In contrast when Kitrina plays in Brussels she has got used to her hostess arranging barbecues and other events at which Kitrina is expected to share her faith.

While playing as an amateur, Kitrina found it difficult to relate her faith to her golf. When she started to play as a professional she became aware of one or two other Christian players. Through a sequence of events Kitrina felt God was leading her to set up a fellowship group.

"My sister sent me a book by George Verwer, the director of Operation Mobilization, an international Christian mission, about being a leader in your field. Then, on one Sunday that I happened to be in Bristol, Nduka Odizor, the Nigerian tennis player, turned up at Christchurch, Clifton, with Fritz Glaus who travels on the men's tennis circuit as a Christian friend of the players. Fritz told me about the twice-weekly fellowship meeting. So I thought that the Lord was really speaking to me about it. Previous to that I had had various chats with Jane Connachan and I'd always felt really uplifted when I spoke to her about the Lord, so I asked if she would be interested in meeting regularly as Christians. Jane was very keen. Moreover Alison Nicholas had just become a Christian so it really started with the three of us."

This was in 1985 and the group has gone from strength to strength over the years. At present the meetings are atended by about 10 to 15 players.

Over the years several players have come to faith through the witness of the group. Players from different countries – England, Scotland, USA, Sri Lanka, South Africa – and from any number of denominational backgrounds have come together and illustrated the truth of being all one in Christ Jesus.

In 1989 the players started an annual residential get-together. In 1990 the subject of baptism came up. Three of the players, Alison Nicholas, Jane Connachan and Tiru Fernando, thought about it, prayed about it and decided they ought to be baptised. A service of baptism was hastily arranged at Kensington Temple in London the following day.

One of the early meetings which took place at the Matchplay tournament at Bramall in Cheshire was attended only by Jane Connachan and Kitrina. What added spice to the occasion was that Jane was to play Kitrina in the quarter-final the following day. At the meeting, Jane prayed about the match, that God would be glorified and that people watching would know that they were Christians by the way they played the match. Jane won their match and went on to win the tournament.

The fellowship group has been a great help to Kitrina. "One of the biggest problems facing me during my first year on tour was that I wasn't getting much teaching or fellowship. Due to the nature of golf, we are often travelling or playing on Sundays. For some Christians, having to work on the Sabbath would be unacceptable. But each of us faces the question of what we will and will not do on Sundays. My ideal Sunday would be spent worshipping and studying. However, I think every one of us should look to God and not to others about these things. For this reason I do play on Sundays. For me, the day itself is irrelevant. It is the time that is important. I prayed about the fact that I felt like a spiritual gypsy, about how I felt I was missing the guidance, fellowship and support which are part of the structure of a normal Christian life. My needs were first met through my sister, Karen, who kept me supplied with books, tapes and the odd earful when she thought I needed a rebuke. I also kept bumping into mature Christians on my travels. On buses, trains, aeroplanes, in fact in the most odd places I would often find someone to talk to."

In recent years Kitrina's sister Karen has moved from being spiritual adviser and encourager to Kitrina to being an unofficial pastor to Christian women golfers. Through the generosity of Kensington Temple – Karen's employers at the time, who released her for 20 days a year – she was able to travel on the tour in the same way that Fritz Glaus, whom Kitrina had met years previously, does on the tennis tour.

Kitrina is a person of contasts. No one works harder at her game, yet she is far from obsessed with it. Writing about the British amateur in 1982, John Hennessy of *The*

Times described her as "an attractive personality with the ability to switch suddenly between smiling relaxation to severe dedication on the course". As this was probably the first time Hennessy had become aware of Kitrina, it was an astute observation and one from which Kitrina is very recognisable.

She has trained herself not to notice who is in the gallery and to shut out anything which might distract her from the job in hand. Yet if something funny happens she will collapse in a fit of hysterical laughter.

A few years ago I was watching her play against Dale Reid in a matchplay tournament. At a crucial stage she struck a 7-iron from 120 yard and it flew straight into the hole. In an instant she turned towards me saying, "Stuart, don't make your praying so obvious!"

Away from the golf course, there are loads of things that Kitrina likes doing. "My ideal day off," she jokes, "would be to go scuba diving in the morning on the barrier reef and to be taken up in a fighter plane in the afternoon." She also likes "taking pictures, walking in forests, beautiful scenery, driving, listening to music, cooking, eating, going to movies. I love having the whole family together. We have great laughs." Kitrina also enjoys painting, regarding her paintings as "all right but I wouldn't ever sell any of them".

One summer she built a patio in the garden of the house which she shares with her mother just outside Bristol, overlooking the Bristol Channel. It was a mammoth task as it involved raising the level of that part of the garden several feet. A fellow professional golfer told me with a shrug, "Kitrina always tries to find something new to learn each winter."

Kitrina adds without a hint of arrogance, "I am fortunate in that I seem to be able to do anything I really want to. I could have been a painter, a musician, an actress. The Lord has blessed me with a talent to be good at anything I put my mind to."

When you talk to people who know Kitrina well, the words that keep cropping up are "determination, discipline, concentration, a born leader". One friend said, "You never win an argument with Kitrina." She doesn't waste a second and crams more into the day than anyone I know. In 1990 while playing in the Variety Club Classic in Reading – she led the tournament for the first three days – she was up to her eyes in the organisation of the Christians in Sport golf day the following Monday and her own birthday party on the Sunday the tournament finished. She seemed to thrive on the pressure. When I asked for some time to talk about this chapter she suggested 7am in Reading – about half-way for both of us. She was on her way to a golf day, clinic and fashion show.

Mitchell Platts (*The Times*) has written of her that she learned at an early stage "that there could be no substitute for hard work".

About six years ago she got involved in Christians in Sport, serving on its National Executive Committee for several years. The annual Christians in Sport golf day, which is held to bring together golfers of all standards and to raise money for Christians in Sport, was Kitrina's idea. She also organises it almost single-handed.

One person who has had a significant part in Kitrina's successes is Gus Thomas, her boyfriend and on many occasions caddy. Women in professional sport often find it difficult to sustain relationships. The boyfriend or husband has either to lead an independent life and accept long absences or to travel with her as an appendage. Husbands who caddy for their wives have at times put the relationship under considerable pressure when a criticism expressed in the heat and tension of the moment is carried over into the relationship.

Gus and Kitrina have seemed comfortable with either role. Gus has at times caddied for her full-time, and as a county-standard player himself is able to give her great assistance on the golf course. Lately he has been pursuing a course in quantity surveying and caddying when he can get away. Kitrina says, "Gus is my best friend. We like being together. We are the same on the golf course as we are on the beach or at the shops."

Golf writer Lewine Mair says she knows no golfer, other than possibly Gary Player, who has used every ounce of talent more than Kitrina.

The last word goes to Kitrina, who summed up her mission in her essay "Women in Sport" in *Women to Women* (MARC, 1988): "I can now see that God has placed me in golf for many purposes. It wasn't by luck or by chance. Jesus said, 'Go into all the world and preach the good news to all creation' (Mark 16:15). This doesn't mean just in Third-World countries. What about our towns, villages, neighbours? I believe God puts Christians in all walks of life – in offices, factories, as doctors, dentists, road sweepers, pilots, in sports, music and the arts . . . If we all go overseas, who will tell people around us the Good News – the people in the queue at the supermarket or living next door?

"A reporter for the *Guardian* once said to me after I'd been talking to her about Jesus, 'Kitrina, if you feel this way, why don't you become a missionary?' I replied, 'I am one.'"

CAREER SUMMARY

Amateur

1980   Gloucestershire champion
1981   Gloucestershire champion
       Scottish Girls' Open Stroke play champion
1982   Gloucestershire champion
       British Amateur champion
       Portuguese Amateur champion
       Cotswold Hills Gold Vase winner
1983   Gloucestershire champion
1984   Gloucestershire champion

Professional

Tournament wins

1984   Ford Ladies' Classic
       Hoganas Swedish Open
1986   Mitsubishi Colt Cars Jersey Open
1987   Hennessy Cognac Ladies' Cup
1989   St Moritz Ladies' Classic
       Godiva European Masters

European Order of Merit (ranking):

1984   2nd
1985   7th
1986   12th
1987   7th
1988   9th
1989   3rd
1990   11th

Other

Teams:

1982   Curtis Cup (Britain v USA)
1983   European Team Championship
1987   England Professional

Holes in One in competitive golf: 3

JONATHAN EDWARDS

Jonathan Edwards jumped into the public eye because he refused to compete on Sunday. The occasion was the Track and Field Olympic trials in August 1988.

Jonathan's event, the Triple Jump, was scheduled in May to take place on the Sunday. Immediately he informed the selectors who had decreed that the first two in each event would be automatically selected, that he would not be taking part. Although only ranked fourth in Great Britain at that time he decided to bank on securing the one discretionary place. The decision made the headlines in most of the national newspapers and the relatively unknown triple jumper found himself hailed as the new Eric Liddell.

The question of Sunday sport remains high on the British agenda. Attempts to change the laws affecting Sunday trading, and thus sport, are contentiously debated in Parliament. The Keep Sunday Special campaign commands a lot of support from churches across the country. Many who are not churchgoers lobby their local politicians to preserve the "traditional British Sunday".

Perhaps the greatest boost of all came from the success of the film *Chariots of Fire*. David Puttnam's Oscar-winning movie came out in 1980, and told the story of two gold medal winning athletes at the Olympic Games in Paris in 1924.

Harold Abrahams was the Ben Johnson of his era. The comparison is not intended to be slanderous. Like

Johnson, Abrahams was explosively fast over 100 metres, and like Ben Johnson he used methods which at least raised eyebrows. Johnson, of course, was sensationally disqualified for using drugs to win the 100 metres at the Seoul Olympics in 1988. Abrahams employed a professional coach but held on to his gold medal.

Scotsman Eric Liddell was portrayed in the film as the true amateur. He trained alone on the Scottish hills, he played rugby for his country, spent his spare time preaching in schools and churches and eventually sailed for China to die as a missionary in 1945.

Above all Liddell is presented as the man who would not run on a Sunday. So great is his devotion to the Sabbath that, in one famous scene, he informs the Prince of Wales as courteously as he can that his devotion to the King of Kings must overrule even obedience to his monarch. Liddell's problem was that the 100 metres heats were scheduled for a Sunday. The film dramatises history, suggesting that this was only announced as the ferry set sail for France with the British team. In fact, as in Edwards' case, Liddell knew well in advance. He scratched from the 100 metres, won a bronze medal in the 200 metres and against all the odds won the 400 metres gold medal, an event at which he was a relative novice.

Jonathan Edwards' story does not yet have this fairy tale element, but the comparisons are obvious. Certainly until 1991 Jonathan was very much an amateur. He, like Liddell, comes from a strong Christian background, where Sabbath observance was mandatory. He consistently refused to compete or train on a Sunday, risking non-selection for his country by so doing. He, like Liddell, became an Olympian.

The comparison may well not end there. It would be a surprise to no one if Jonathan's athletics career were followed by full-time Christian service of some kind or other. No doubt Jonathan thinks a Barcelona gold medal would complete the story nicely!

At school in the West Country the young Edwards showed all-round ability at sports. Initially he distinguished himself as a footballer, and then in Secondary school at rugby and cricket. He represented his school first team in both sports. This left little time for athletics, and so it was not until he went to Durham University to study physics that his outstanding skill at the triple jump began to emerge.

Jonathan's father, Andy, a Church of England vicar, plays an important role at this point. Without doing much training Jonathan had won the 1984 Schools Athletics Championship which he entered as a "bit of fun". At Durham he won a couple of triple jump competitions and Andy, sensing his son's potential, made contact with Carl Johnson, the North-East based athletics coach, and asked him to add Jonathan to his squad. As he looks back, Jonathan says he knew that athletics was the sport in which he was most likely to succeed but "Dad pushed me" and for that he is grateful.

It was a very loving, protective and disciplined background from which he emerged. Jonathan cannot remember the time when he became a Christian. His mother tells him that when he was six years old he gave his life to Jesus. Since then, he says, "the Christian life has been getting to know God and finding Him faithful and trustworthy."

As the Olympic Games of 1988 approached, Jonathan was not the only British athlete facing the dilemma of whether or not to compete on Sunday. Long jumper Barrington Williams, a lay preacher from Chesterfield, also made it clear to the selectors that he would not be available for the long jump because the qualifying rounds in Seoul were scheduled for a Sunday.

Williams' career in athletics must be one of the most extraordinary in the long history of track and field. At the age of 18 he longed to be a professional footballer. Playing in an amateur game one Sunday, he felt God telling him that he should not be on the playing fields on the Sabbath. At half-time he walked off the field and he has never taken part in Sunday sport since.

For the next ten years he competed half-heartedly in long jump and sprinting events at county and club level. He was noticeable for his ability and his lack of training. He found that he rarely felt inclined or motivated to do more than one evening's training each week. At the age of thirty he emerged on the international scene simply because he was so good. From the outset he made it clear that he had no intention of altering either his training routines or his attitude to Sunday.

So when in 1988, at the advanced age of 32, he became a serious contender for selection for the Great Britain long jump team, it was a great disappointment to discover that the competition in Seoul would be on a Sunday. He immediately made himself unavailable. However, this unique athlete did not stop there. He decided to give the 100 metres a go and duly qualified for the team by coming third at the trials behind Linford Christie and John Regis.

When he got to Korea he made quite sure that he experienced as much of the Christian revival going on in the country as possible. He made great friends with Christian volunteers working in the village. He attended Christian churches across Seoul, and was a regular at the gatherings in the Village chapel.

When it actually got to the running he continued his unpredictable style. He qualified well in the first heat wearing a favourite old pair of spikes. In the second heat he thought he ought to wear his new spikes, provided by a sponsor, because the race was live on television. They were very uncomfortable and he ran a poor time to be eliminated. He was disappointed but told me with typical good humour, "I think God's got other plans for me out here."

Sixteen months later he was selected for the long jump at the Commonwealth Games in Auckland. The event was not on a Sunday and so he had no problem in going. Unfortunately he no-jumped every time and was dreadfully disappointed. "I felt sure," he said, "that if I could get it right just once I'd be up in the medals." His coaches and his fellow athletes shook their heads in frustration. They all felt sure that if he trained more he would lessen the risk of missing the board and no-jumping. But Barrington is a unique character, and his presence as a friend and pastor is appreciated by many in the British team.

I recall in Auckland his kindness to Matt Belsham, a young British pole-vaulter attending his first major international event. Barrington took him under his wing and escorted him around Auckland. Though I must say, Barrington, are you sure horse-riding the day before your event was really the best preparation?

Jonathan Edwards is a remarkably uncomplicated and straightforward character compared to Barrington. They arrived on the international scene at about the same time and have usually shared a room together in training camps and at meets. They have become great friends. Jonathan remarks that he imagines they were put together originally because the authorities thought it would be best if the "religious maniacs" were segregated.

Of course, it had the opposite affect. Such an encouragement have they been to each other and to the growing number of other Christians in the British Track and Field team that there is now no way the authorities can marginalise the Christians even if they wanted to. In fact, the team management has consistently been co-operative with the requests of the athletes to hold fellowship meetings and Bible studies and be supported by chaplains at events.

In Seoul Jonathan performed well below his best. This was his first Great Britain International appearance and he found himself jumping against people he had only seen before on television. To qualify he had cleared 16.76 metres, but in Seoul his best effort was only 15.88 metres and he failed to progress beyond the preliminary stage. It was all a bit of an anti-climax, especially when neither of his team-mates, fellow-Christian Vernon Samuels (16:28) nor Jonathan Herbert (16:18) qualified.

But the experience of the Games fired Jonathan's enthusiasm. The previous year he had come ninth in the World Student Games in Zagreb and that had given him a taste for big-time athletics. The training camps in Japan which preceded the Olympics and the whole experience of a brilliantly organised Olympiad convinced him that he should take his athletics career more seriously. "I came to see my talent as a gift from God," he said, "and I wanted to try and keep using it for Him."

To be physically at your fittest and emotionally charged up to do your best is a thrill for any young athlete. To discover that there is a group of team mates who share your spiritual goals as well is a tremendous bonus. That is what happened to the Christian athletes during that Olympic trip. They saw the purposes of God in their athletic ability.

For many people who watched the Olympics, the abiding memory will be the sight of the disgraced Ben Johnson being ushered to the airport on the way home to Toronto just a few hours after winning the fastest 100 metres race in history from Carl Lewis and Linford Christie. The scandal of drug-taking hung over all the reports that emanated from Seoul. But for the competitors it was quite different. For the first time in 16 years there was almost total representation at the Games. In 1976 the black countries did not go to Montreal. In 1980 the Americans boycotted Moscow and in 1984 the Eastern Bloc countries boycotted Los Angeles. In Seoul, at last, they all got together.

There were some unforgettable moments: Florence Griffith-Joyner winning the 200 metres, the Kenyans dominating the middle distance races, the Korean boxer refusing to leave the ring after being beaten, Daley Thompson breaking his pole vault during the decathlon and the whole Olympic stadium crowd catching its breath together.

In the Village most athletes simply described the atmosphere and organisation as "magic". It was a great experience for everyone and it persuaded Jonathan that he should try to do as well as he could for the next few years, and certainly until 1992 in Barcelona. He could reassess the situation then.

By his own admission he only began to train seriously after the Olympics. 1989 turned out to be a great year for him. He reaped the rewards of training five nights a week.

But initially there was trauma. He missed the epic Europa Cup competition in Gateshead because the Triple Jump was on the Sunday. He insists that making himself unavailable was not a big decision at all. Unlike most athletic events, the Europa Cup and the World Cup, which follows it, are team events. Each athlete earns points for his team as well as individual medals. What would Jonathan have thought if his absence had cost the Great Britain team vital points? "I would have been very disappointed," he says. "But I would have felt at peace with myself because I had my priorities right in putting God first."

His place in the team was taken by his great friend and fellow-Christian Vernon Samuels, whose personal best is some way behind Jonathan's. As it turned out, the Great Britain team never looked back from the great start Kriss Akabusi gave them by winning the 400 metres hurdles, and came out clear winners to qualify for the World Cup in Barcelona.

That competition provided the highlight of Jonathan's career up to that point. He leapt an astonishing personal best 17.28 metres to secure 6 points and third place in the competition. It was also the third best jump ever by a Briton and means that the British record by the legendary Keith Connor of 17.57 could be within his reach.

The sad side of the decision not to compete at Gateshead was that Samuels, having been part of a great victory, was omitted from the team to go to Barcelona. The two friends have often discussed how they feel about this. Samuels has no problem with Sunday competition, and takes the same view as Kriss Akabusi, that the 24-hour period which is called the Sabbath in the Bible was given as part of the covenant to the Jews. In the new covenant our Sabbath rest is to be found in Jesus . . . seven days a week. It is a subject over which Christians in every walk of life disagree. The striking thing about the Christians in the Great Britain Track and Field team is that, even though the Sunday issue is a very real one, they remain unified and very supportive of one another.

While Akabusi disagrees with Edwards and vice versa, they both acknowledge the personal legitimacy of the other's view. On Sunday 24th September, 1988, Jonathan, having completed his event in Seoul, attended church and relaxed. Kriss was on the track trying to win a medal in the 4×400 metres relay. Jonathan got to the stadium just in time to cheer on his friend, for he says he's happy to watch sport on a Sunday, especially if his Christian friends are competing. When in December 1990 Jonathan married Alison whom he had met in the worship group at church, Akabusi, Williams and Samuels were very near the top of the guest list.

Jonathan's strict attitude to Sunday is partly the result of his upbringing, partly for sound biblical reasons and partly pragmatic. From the earliest days his family kept Sunday special. He would relax after church, write letters or read a book. During school and university it was not only sport that was "out", he never did any academic work on Sunday either, though one suspects that that was less of a sacrifice. He feels strongly that the "Sabbath was made for man" and that God intended men and women to set aside one special day of the week to concentrate their attention on Him. The early Christians met on the first day of the week, shifting the Sabbath from the Saturday, when the Jews observed it, to Sunday, the day of Jesus' resurrection. On that day they prayed together, taught one another from the Scriptures, encouraged one another in fellowship and broke bread and drank wine to remember the death of Jesus. For Jonathan these things are absolutely basic to the Christian life and he would sooner miss out on an Olympic medal than sacrifice what he sees as a biblical principle.

But there is also a practical reason, he feels, for keeping Sunday separate: "You need one day off each week even if you are not a Christian. Life in Britain is fast paced and you need time to relax and enjoy other people's company." Sunday is a day for recharging the batteries – physically, emotionally and spiritually.

It would be quite wrong to picture Jonathan Edwards,

or Barrington Williams, for that matter, as bigots enforcing their view of Sunday somewhat selfishly on other people. Neither of them insists that his under-standing of Sunday observance is obligatory for all Christians. It is just that after thinking it through this is how they personally feel they must act.

At times both are irritated by the media's concentration on their attitude to Sunday rather than their commitment to Jesus. This was particularly the case in Seoul, where Barrington especially was besieged by requests for interviews. They are always anxious to point out that they are first and foremost believers in Jesus, and their attitude to Sunday flows from that. Time and again the media have portrayed them as "never on a Sunday" athletes, whose religious scruples rule their lives. It is an inaccurate understanding. They both long that Jesus, not rules, should govern their lives; it is just that they choose to use their Sundays in a particular way so as to stay close to the Lord.

The Commonwealth Games came at a difficult time for the British athletes. It is hard to sustain fitness for 12 months and January is usually a time of relaxation. Jonathan was not able to maintain the high standard of the previous summer but won a silver medal in Auckland with a best jump of 16.93 metres. It looked, in fact, as if he had done enough to win gold, but the Cypriot Hadjian-dreou pipped him with a leap of 16.95 metres at his last attempt.

But this trip "down under" was the opportunity for the Christian athletes to build on the foundations laid in Japan and Korea in 1988. For several weeks they trained in Australia, and Jonathan became involved with a youth group at a local church. He loved the enthusiasm and response of the young believers and began to feel that perhaps one day God would use him in full-time ministry.

That was not to be for a while, though. He returned to his job in Newcastle, working for the National Health Service in the regional genetics advisory service, although he hastens to point out that he did not even know what a chromosome was when he got the job. It provided a vital source of income for him and valuable work experience, but he found it hard not to hide his lack of enthusiasm. From January 1991 he decided to work only 10 to 15 hours a week and concentrate more on his training.

The year 1990 had been a frustrating one for him. He had injured himself taking his final jump in Auckland and never really got into the summer season. He felt a little disillusioned and managed only a best jump of 16.84 metres. Perhaps the truth is that he was finding it hard to combine planning for marriage to Alison with work in the laboratory and training.

By 1991 he was happily married, less pressured at work and looking confidently to the future. Unfortunately the schedule for the World Championships in Tokyo put the Triple Jump on the Sunday so it was the domestic season that was occupying his attention. He was horrified to discover that the finals for the Triple Jump in Barcelona were scheduled for a Monday; almost certainly the qualifiers would be on the Sunday. Would his hope of an Olympic medal be dashed at the first hurdle? It was a great relief to discover that the qualifying rounds would be on the Saturday with the Sunday as a day off. It seemed like a great answer to his prayers and helped rekindle his enthusiasm.

So he is looking ahead with great confidence to the future. I asked him if Keith Connor's record was his main target. He seemed surprised at the question. "I just want to do as well as I can, and use what God has given me," he replied disarmingly, "and if the record comes along the way that will be fine."

CAREER SUMMARY

Medals, Achievements etc.
1990   Commonwealth Silver Medal
1989   World Cup Bronze Medal
        UK Champion
        AAA Champion
1988   Seoul Olympics
1987   World Student Games

Progression
1984   15:01 m
1985   14:99 m
1986   16:05 m
1987   16:35 m
1988   16:79 m
1989   17:28 m
1990   16:93 m
1991   17.36 m

Other P.B.'s
100   10.63 s/10.6 – wind assisted
200   22.2 s
LJ   7:23 m

MIKIE HEATON-ELLIS

We had arranged to meet up at Junction 15 of the M4. It was only 6.55am on a chill autumn morning. I followed his big BMW – a gift from a grateful Arab employer – through Marlborough, where a hoot from the horn had the local newsagent running out of his shop with the morning paper. The sun was just rising as we drove up the hill on to Salisbury Plain and into the racing-stables at East Eversleigh. He quickly assembled his wheelchair and hauled himself into it – no fuss.

"I'll give you a lift on the bike," he shouted across to me.

His boss Richard Hannon, a former drummer with pop group The Trogs, was already in the Landrover and the "first lot" were moving out of the yard. The "bike" is a Honda four-wheeler, converted to hand controls, and it goes across more or less any terrain.

Up on the gallops he watched each horse intently, exchanging knowledgeable remarks with the lads as they rode by and Richard Hannon, whose terriers had disappeared down rabbit holes a quarter of a mile away, incurring their master's plainly expressed wrath.

It was an ordinary morning for Mikie Heaton-Ellis. He's paralysed from the chest down and he trains race-horses.

Every sportsman and sportswoman dreads injury. They all know that at any moment their ambitions could be over and their livelihood ended. Every sport is littered with casualties. Jump jockeys are a case in point. There is no sport much more dangerous than riding in National Hunt races. Falling is inevitable.

Every rider's nightmare became Michael Heaton-Ellis's reality on 24th October, 1981. He was riding Dunrose in a steeplechase at Huntingdon, watched by his girlfriend. The irony was that he had "stopped" the horse in its previous race so that it would still be a novice at the start of the 1981 season. Stopping horses (deliberately riding them so that they will not win), though officially frowned upon, is not uncommon. The idea is to keep a horse in an inferior class so that when it wins, thus gaining promotion, it wins a race worth a lot of money. Mikie insists he would not do it now that he is a Christian. They had completed one circuit of the course and as they approached a fence another horse swerved in front of them, causing Dunrose to get too close and blocking Mikie's view. Horse and rider crashed through the top of the fence, and another horse fell onto Mikie as he lay on the ground. His back was broken and he has never walked since.

Mikie enjoyed and thanks God for a secure, happy and privileged childhood. His father was in the Army and Mikie, the oldest of three children, was born in Germany on the 22nd May, 1958. Like many army families the Heaton-Ellises were always on the move so Michael was sent to boarding school at the age of eight. His memories are happy ones. At prep school and later at public school at Radley, just outside Oxford, he developed into a useful all-round sportsman. He captained Radley at rackets, which he loved. He represented the school at cross-country running, 1500 metres and cricket. In fact, he was good enough to represent Southampton University, where he studied Classics, at both cross-country and cricket. "I was a batsman," he says proudly.

But above all he loved horses. His father, an abidingly influential figure in his life, rode in one-day events and hunted the Royal Artillery hounds. Mikie was given his first pony, Beaumont, when he was seven and competed like many youngsters in local gymkhanas during the school holidays. The talk in the Heaton-Ellis household was often of horses. His brother David has become a professional polo player, but in the early days it was hunting and eventing that took priority. Racing was another world and remained largely unexplored until Michael's undergraduate days.

Religion was also kept at arm's length. Like many public school boys Mikie believed in God, got confirmed, and did not resent compulsory attendance at chapel. But he has no recollection of anyone telling him about the possibility of a relationshp with God, and indeed even of the concept of being committed as a Christian. Michael was a reasonably decent, fun-loving Englishman who believed in God and went to church from time to time – "Surely that's what a Christian is?" he thought.

It is very easy to dismiss the kind of Christian education he received from his family and public school as being like an inoculation – "just enough of the disease to stop you catching the real thing". But that would be unfair. Like many who have had seeds of faith sown in them in this way, Mikie found that when things got bad he knew enough to think about God.

Between school and university he entered the army on a short service limited commission (SSLC). Conveniently he found himself stationed at Larkhill on Salisbury Plain riding the "Gunner" horses. He had already, while a schoolboy, ridden a point-to-point winner at Twesledown, and his talent at horsemanship was being noted. The army course that he was sent on at Plymouth in the summer of 1977 was tough – he was in 29 Commando Regiment and they got him fit.

He remembers with surprise that during that highly intensive course he read his Bible and some explanatory notes he had picked up somewhere every day. He recalls that it was out of duty! "Perhaps if I read the Bible God will help me through the course," he thought to himself.

He went to Southampton University as the envy of all students with the relative financial security of an army scholarship. He had the time and the resources to make the best use of the next three years and he wasted none of it.

These years constituted the active riding career of Mikie Heaton-Ellis. On Sir Jaffa he enjoyed some successful forays into eventing, qualifying for the prestigious Badminton Horse Trials just one week before his fateful accident. His best result was in 1979 when he came ninth in the International Class at Wylie Horse Trials. He also managed to ride 11 National Hunt winners in steeplechases and competed in a few flat races as well.

He vividly recalls one weekend when he rode in an amateur flat race at Kempton Park on the Friday, a Novice steeplechases at Stratford on the Saturday, and an advanced one-day event in Devon on the Sunday! The latter was possible thanks to a girlfriend who had lovingly gone on ahead to get the horse ready. On Monday he was due in court in Bristol to testify on behalf of one of his soldiers – "I was a bit late," he laughs.

What all this adds up to is an outstanding horseman having a whale of a time! His social life was pretty exciting too. There were plenty of pretty young students only too happy to be seen with the glamorous young army officer. He was good-looking, athletic, amusing, intelligent and relatively rich. He enjoyed the occasional student prank as well. He had a flirtatious interest in

Tory politics and in a strongly left-wing university successfully campaigned for election to the influential student committee on a "Vote sport, Vote Heaton-Ellis" ticket. He promised all and sundry in the sports club that he would increase the size of their grants from central funds and so secured the votes of all the sporty students. He confesses he hardly ever turned up for meetings subseqeuntly and was sacked from the committee in due course.

For many years he used to say he had taken part in a student demonstration when a group of Conservative students, dressed in very smart suits, sat at a table in Trafalgar Square handing out leaflets about getting more money for pensioners, eating caviar and drinking champagne. All around them the "lefties" were shouting slogans and campaigning for higher student grants. In fact it was a group of Mikie's friends who engaged in the demonstration, and only after he became a Christian did he admit he had not been involved at all.

If you were from his background and enjoyed his interests you would quite reasonably have concluded that the pre-accident Mikie Heaton-Ellis was "a hell of a good lad". If you weren't, then you would probably have thought he was a "rich young fool".

Oddly perhaps, Mikie himself says he was always aware that something was missing from his life. He appeared, and was, outwardly very successful. But on his own he would often wonder about life: "What is it all about? Is the army really where I want to be? Why do I feel a tension all the time?"

These are not, of course, earth-shattering questions. What student has not asked them? It is mentioned here because it would be wrong to think of Mikie as a feckless gadabout. He is intelligent and sensitive. His 2:1 degree in Classics required some hard work, and the brokenhearted girlfriends he left behind were not ditched selfishly or carelessly.

He left Southampton intent on serving his five years in the army, before concentrating on riding and training race-horses. He instructed his parents, who answered the telephone at home, to accept every ride he was offered. He was full of hopes, ambitions and talent.

And then came Huntingdon . . .

The ambulance rushed a semi-conscious Mikie to Addenbrookes Hospital in Cambridge and after a few days he was transferred to the spinal injury unit at Stoke Mandeville. He can remember little about the accident itself or the few days that immediately followed. He recalls pain and anger. He was shocked to learn later that he had refused treatment from an Asian doctor, and not allowed a black orderly to touch him! He had never considered himself racially prejudiced, but a dark side was emerging.

He remembers being totally confident that God would heal him. After all, everything else had gone right in his life up to this point. He had achieved what he set out to do, and now walking again was just the next challenge. It angered him that the doctors gave him no hope at all. He did not believe them when they told him that his injuries were permanent. He was in control of his life. He always had been. This was merely a temporary set-back. There were no tears, no remorse, no self-pity. Visitors left feeling uplifted by his courage. "Isn't Mikie wonderful," they would say, "so brave and so positive." One girlfriend arrived when Mikie's father was with him; she took one look at the patient and said, "I don't know what to say," then burst into tears and fled. "Well, I didn't do very well there, did I!" commented Mikie.

One great sadness was that his girlfriend, who had been with him at Huntingdon, understandably could not cope with what had happened and the relationship ended. Mikie stayed at Stoke Mandeville for 10 months, determined not to leave unless he could do so on his feet. Eventually he did, but only with the help of crutches and callipers.

Along with all the heroic personal effort came a great deal of prayer. Mikie appreciated this – he was prepared to try anything in order to walk again. His parents got churches praying. He was aware of the Lord's strength coming to him through some Christian friends. There was one who was especially helpful. Ralph Crathorne had been a close friend in the army and he had a special role to play in Mikie's story a few years later.

He wasn't so sure about one group of Christians who came up from Salisbury and crowded around his bed, laying hands on him and praying in strange languages. He was desperately embarrassed and couldn't wait for them to leave. Now he laughs about it because he has come to understand about the gifts of tongues and how it can be used.

By August 1982 he had learnt to look after himself and was ready to leave hospital. He was grateful to Stoke Mandeville and admires all their efforts for him, but he was never an easy patient and was exasperated by their pessimism. Out in the real world he felt sure things would improve.

He got a job at Newmarket at the Thoroughbred Breeders' Association, and for two years travelled around the stud farms and sales of Britain's flat-racing industry. He was converted totally to flat-racing. By the end of that two years he knew that what he wanted to do was train these beautiful thoroughbred young horses to be the best and fastest they could be. He loved their speed and athleticism. He had, he discoverd, got an eye for a horse ("It's a gift from the Lord," he says). Though confined to a wheelchair he had discovered a sport in which he would play a full and active part.

And, of coure, the paralysis was only temporary anyway! He attended healing services, and encouraged everyone he could to go on praying for him.

"It didn't make a scrap of difference," he says.

He met and fell in love with a beautiful Irish painter called Katie. Together they would climb the mountain that his injury represented. In 1984 at their wedding in Harlow they embarked together on a crusade with the object of getting Mikie back on his feet. Neither of them put it like this at the time, but Mikie knows that that was what it was about really. The bridegroom struggled down the aisle on crutches, and stood up at the reception to receive the guests. For weeks he had refused all alcohol in order to be physically fit enough to cope with the physical exertions of the wedding. Even at the reception there was only tonic water in his glass! And Mikie had always enjoyed a drink or two.

In reality the marriage was doomed from the start. Katie now says that she knew immediately that it would not work. The sexual problems they faced were enormous and Mikie was realising that the healing that was going on was all about his mental attitudes and not his body. This was no comfort to Katie. In August 1987 she left.

For two years they had lived in a cottage in Sussex and Mikie had worked as John Dunlop's assistant at the training stable at beautiful Arundel Castle. He knew he could train winners and he loved the work. Towards the end of the marriage Sheik Mohammed Al-Maktoum, one of the famous brothers whose love of racing is legendary, and the biggest race-horse owner in the world with 500 horses in training, offered Mikie the lucrative job of being his racing manager.

His particular job was to place the sheik's horses in the right races. This meant careful liaison with the trainers. It was a wonderful apprenticeship for the aspiring trainer. He saw the best men and women all over the world working with their horses, and learnt the complicated business of getting the right horse in the right race.

Very few young trainers have travelled the world like Mikie has, and always he watched, asked questions and learned. Very importantly, too, in the small world of thoroughbred racing, he got to know everyone, and just as crucially got known – after all, there weren't many people in wheelchairs at race meetings and on the gallops. The lifestyle suited Mikie. He had his hand-controlled BMW and carphone. He jetted around the world, always staying in the best hotels, with a group of glamorous women around him. If you can ever say it of someone paralysed from the chest down, life was good.

The marriage break-up left him shattered. "If God thinks this is going to make me turn to Him, He's wrong," he told his father angrily. He knew God was there and he was sick of the unfair game He was playing with him. His ego had always been dinstinctly sizeable, and desertion by a wife had left him feeling humiliated.

At Newbury races he chatted up a good-looking Californian and swallowed her sob story of parents killed in a car crash and looking for a new life. He fixed her up with a job in Newbury, and then discovered to his horror that she had duped him totally. She was only 15 and had run away from home. He was feeling pretty sorry for himself one Saturday night in Newmarket, when his old friend Ralph Crathorne and his wife, Cally, came to stay.

As Mikie says, "The word of the Lord came to me that weekend in Newmarket." As they talked, initially about the fool Mikie had made of himself with the Californian girl, he came to see that his sin was not just a question of the wrong things he did, but of alienation from God. He had been angry at God since the accident, but now he saw that God, much more reasonably, was angry at him. He had been the centre of his world, thinking of God only as a "sugar Daddy in the sky" whose job it was to be at his beck and call. He had treated God rather as he had treated the girls who got his horses ready at Southampton University – as a servant. Now he saw that life was really about serving God. He had had it all upside-down.

Ralph explained that God loved Mikie, that he had sent His Son Jesus to end the awful alienation by dying for Mikie on a cross. He could be God's friend, God would never desert him or let him down. Furthermore Jesus had risen from the dead. He was alive today, and He longed for Mikie to commit his life to Him.

It's amazing how things work. The next day Mikie had arranged to go and have supper with the vicar who had married Katie and him in Harlow. After the evening service the vicar again explained what was now clear to Mikie as the "way of salvation". The vicar sensibly left Mikie to go and make up his own mind, but explained what steps he should take. He made it simple:

A – Admit that he was a sinner, and needed God.
B – Believe that Jesus, the perfect Son of God, had died on the Cross so he could be forgiven.
C – Count the cost of the following Jesus – He must be in control from then on.
D – Decide by an act of will to follow Jesus.

Mikie's heart was beating fast as he sat alone in his room that night, looked through the Bible references Ralph and the vicar had given him, and prayed that Jesus would take over his life.

And, my word, He really has!

Initially, as it is for many people, Mikie "felt" very

little. In fact he says that he prayed that prayer of commitment repeatedly over the next few days in order to make sure it was real. There were many things he was unsure about and his understanding was not at all complete. He knew that he was truly sorry for leaving God out for so long and failing to surrender to Him. But he also recognises that a powerful motivation in becoming a Christian was the hope that God would now help him more obviously. In particular he thought it reasonable to expect that God would bring Katie back, rather as a conjurer produces a rabbit out of a hat. It was not to be.

When challenged that he turned to God because he thought that would be the way to get to walk again, he is adamant that by this time he was accepting the permanency of his disability. He had emerged from his original tunnel of blind optimism. That is not to say that he has no hope left, and some amongst his family still believe fervently that he will walk again, but for Mikie it doesn't seem a problem any more. "There is really nothing you cannot do if you put your mind to it," he told me as he made me coffee in his kitchen. Knowing Mikie you believe him.

He was introduced in Newmarket to the vicar, Roy Rimmer, and congregation of All Saints Church – the "racing church". He felt immediately at home there, and received from Roy a personal course of instruction in the basics of the Christian faith.

Mikie was still working for Sheik Mohammed and was travelling a great deal. Nonetheless, for several months he and Roy met together once a week early in the morning. For Mikie it was all totally new. He found he could understand the Bible, and it made sense of his life and of all the questions he had asked as a young student in Southampton. He learnt how to read the Bible in a constructive way, daily, applying it to his life. He learnt how to pray, and how to talk about his faith. For the first time in many years he began to see a real direction for his life. Perhaps most usefully of all, Roy and he learnt a verse of Scripture by heart each week and tested each other on it.

He still has theological questions which he cannot answer. His eyes filled with tears when he spoke about the "good people I know" who seem to have no chance of going to heaven because they have no relationship with Jesus. "I would love there to be another way," he says, "but I know there cannot be really."

In April 1989 Mikie returned to the track – this time in a wheelchair in the London Marathon. It is quite a story.

Mikie had quickly become an integral part of the Christian family at All Saints. One family in the church had a child, Joe Myers, who had spina bifida. Joe's parents knew that the famous Peto Institute in Hungary could help the boy, but they did not have the resources to pay for treatment. Mikie, typically, decided to help. His first motivation in starting training was to raise the £20,000 Joe needed. In fact, he not only managed to do that but in raising a magnificent total of £59,000 made substantial donations also to the International Spinal Research Trust and the Injured Jockeys' Association.

He also gave money to All Saints so that they could employ a church worker in an outreach ministry to the numerous young people who arrive in Newmarket to work at the studs and racing stables. A young American Christian was taken on and a youth programme begun. Already several of the young people have made commitments to Christ and the work is developing. After all this there was still money enough to establish an All Saints Disaster Fund!

Mikie found training for the Marathon very tough

indeed. He had bought a lightweight racing wheelchair, and he soon became a familiar sight on the roads in Newmarket. Because he had never done a wheelchair marathon before he had to do the qualifying time before his entry could be sanctioned. His first attempt, ironically, was back at the Huntingdon race-course where his riding career had ended eight years before. Everything was fine until about half-way round, where the course went across a rather muddy field. The wheelchair could not cope with it and Mikie took two hours to do two miles. He was exhausted, disillusioned and still well short of the qualifying time.

A week before the final qualification date he was at Leopardstown for a race meeting and decided to stay overnight and have another go in the Dublin marathon. He was pretty desperate – time was running out, and he had severely sore wrists from training. He spent all of Sunday praying and resting. He rang everyone he could think of and asked them to pray, for he was sure that in his own strength he would be unable to complete the race.

After six or seven mile his wrists became unbearably painful. He longed to stop and was close to doing so. But those memorised Bible verses stood him in good stead. It was Philippians chapter 4 verse 13 that he particularly remembers saying over and over again: "I can do anything through him who gives me strength." His time was 3hrs 2mins. In the London Marathon he improved on that and a time of 2hrs 42mins was a great personal triumph. He remembers the whole thing as "a great experience".

So what difference has being a Christian made to Mikie? On the face of it not much has changed. He is still the same cheerful, wholehearted character. He is still in a wheelchair. He still enjoys the company of pretty women. He still loves racing and even has the occasional flutter; though he is anxious to point out that the gambling, for which horse racing is often criticised by Christians, is a very unimportant motivation for him. He is still ambitious to make his mark as a trainer. He still loves to watch and bring on the handsome animals in his charge. He is still fundamentally the same Mikie Heaton-Ellis he was before, but in his heart he knows he is completely different.

Before he lived just for himself, but now he lives for Jesus. He spends time in prayer before every decision. His Bible is even more indispensable each day than the *Racing Post* or the *Sporting Life*. The dynamic force in his life is his relationship with God. He has made sense of his terrible injuries. Rather than spending time thinking about what might have been, he is constantly talking about the things he can now do, which he would never have done but for the accident. He never says that God caused him to fall that awful day at Huntingdon, but he is quite convinced that God has brought and will continue to bring good out of the disaster.

He hopes to see a growing Christian presence in the world of horse-racing. He has already linked up with the Equestrian Christian Fellowship, a branch of Christians in Sport, with contacts mainly in polo and eventing. He also meets regularly with National Hunt Jockey and fellow believer Hywel Davies, who lives not far away from Mikie. He also enjoys participating in Christians in Sport teams which visit schools. He loves to share his faith and has a great hunger to grow in his knowledge of God.

And he has a great plan and a great vision for the future. When I told him of my intention to write this chapter he was reticent at first. He feels he is not yet a winner in his sport. At the time of writing no horse has ever appeared on a card as being trained by Michael Heaton-Ellis, let alone entered the winners' enclosure. Having said that, with Mikie's help, Richard Hannon had the most successful year of his life in 1990, and together they successfully trained Tirol to win the 2,000 guineas at Newmarket. Mikie is typically modest about this. "I am sure he would have had a great year anyway," he laughed. But I could see that there was a lot of personal satisfaction, too.

It may not be long before the name of Heaton-Ellis becomes better known.

If all goes to plan Mike will be training on his own at Barbury Castle Stables, near Marlborough, from the summer of 1991. A local landowner has provided a house, and there are superb gallops all around the estate. Mikie is investing a large amount of capital in a stable yard, office and staff in order to break into the world he loves so much. For the moment his apprenticeship with Richard Hannon, his involvement with a small owners' syndicate whose horses are trained by Barry Hills at Manton, and his planning for the future take all his time. Training race-horses is a labour-intensive and very risky business at the best of times. To give up a well-paid job with Sheik Mohammed and to move to a non-existent yard with no guaranteed income would be regarded by many as foolhardy.

"I prayed very hard about it," says Mikie. "I understood all the dangers, and have had to struggle to work out my motivation for doing this. Was it for me? Was I trying to prove something? Was I being selfish and stupid? The truth is I really feel the Lord's hand is on this plan. I wrote to prospective owners saying just that, "That the Lord had given me Barbury," and they didn't object at all! It's true, though, that if I wasn't a Christian I would be very jittery."

But Mikie Heaton-Ellis is not a foolish, super-spiritual, unworldly Christian embarking on some half-baked scheme. He has learnt his craft carefully, and used the wonderful opportunities the Sheik, John Dunlop and Richard Hannon have given him. He believes he has come up with a method which will work.

"What I want to do is train each horse as an individual," he says. "Hopefully we can identify at an early age the distance that each animal is suited to. I hope to be able to devise a training schedule ideally suited for each horse, rather than train the whole lot in the same way. Furthermore, I've got excellent gallops here – good ground and a wide variety of terrain. I feel that I am where God wants me to be, and I feel that with a good deal of hard work the plan will succeed."

A few short years ago this man was lying paralysed and barely conscious in hospital. Blind optimism assured him he would one day walk again. He hasn't, but not long ago a friend who is not a committed Christian said, "Mikie, I can see that the Lord has made you walk again . . . but not in the way we all thought."

Now he is optimistic again. This time he has good solid reasons for believing that success awaits him in the future. If it does he will use whatever influence he has to build a Christian presence in the world of racing – the world into which he believes God has sent him.

CAREER SUMMARY

1958	Born 22 May 1958
1976–1981	Amateur jockey. Rode 11 National Hunt winners
1979	Eventing: 9th in the International Class, Wylie Horse Trials
1981	Eventing: Qualified for 1982 Badminton Horse Trials 24 October 1981 – accident at Huntingdon which broke his back
1981–1982	October 1981 to August 1982 in Stoke Mandeville Hospital
1982–1984	Assistant Chief Executive: Thoroughbred Breeders' Association, Newmarket
1985–1987	Assistant trainer to John Dunlop, Arundel
1987–1989	Racing manager to Sheik Mohammed Al-Maktoum, the biggest race-horse owner in the world with 500 horses in training
1989	London Marathon (wheelchair) 2 hours 42 minutes
1990–1991	Assistant trainer to Richard Hannon. In 1990 they had 80 winners including in Tirol the winner of the English 2000 Guineas and the Irish 2000 Guineas
	In 1991 25 winners*
	*at June 1991

BRIAN IRVINE

However long he lives, Brian Irvine is unlikely to forget 1990. The year started with him unsure of a place in the Aberdeen football team from week to week. By the time the year ended, he had not only established himself in the first team but had become the hero of Aberdeen's cup-final victory and, at the age of 24, gained his first cap for Scotland. If that wasn't enough, he became a father in September when Donna gave birth to Hannah.

Brian grew up in Airdrie, a town of some 45,000 people, about 15 miles east of Glasgow, the son of a policeman. He progressed through school and youth football. An important influence in those days was Jim McKerley, an officer in the 11th Airdrie company of the Boys' Brigade of which Brian was a member, and his first football manager. "He was a big help in my football and my life. Many a night, though, he must have despaired of us, the things we got up to!" But Brian has never forgotten Jim's influence and is quick to acknowledge his debt to him.

He was playing for a team in Airdrie called Victoria Park when he was seen by a Falkirk scout. Something about Brian clearly impressed the scout and he had a trial with Falkirk.

This resulted in his signing what were called "provisional forms" for Falkirk. This, to be frank, did not mean a great deal. He was tied to Falkirk in the sense that he could not sign for another League club. In practice he continued to play for Victoria Park. In February 1984, however, he played a reserve game for Falkirk, and although the game was abandoned after half an hour, Brian did well enough to be signed on as a part-time professional player. He played in the reserves for the rest of the season. Then he made his League debut on 21st April, 1984, for Falkirk in the Scottish First Division.

It was a home game against Morton which Falkirk lost 1–0. He found himself up against the Scottish international striker, Willie Pettigrew. But he acquitted himself well. The *Falkirk Herald* match report stated: "Defender Brian Irvine, making his debut for the Bairns, did a super marking job on striker Pettigrew, which indicated that he could be a player for the future."

The Falkirk manager, Billy Lamont, was equally pleased with the debutant: "The boy has been showing up well in the reserves. He did well in the first team against Morton. For his size, he is a very mobile player." Brian played two more games for the Falkirk side that finished seventh in the First Division that season.

The following season he held a regular place in the Falkirk team that finished third in the First Division, just missing out on promotion to the Premier Division. A highlight of that season was playing against Rangers in the Skol Cup at Ibrox. Rangers won 1–0 and went on to win the Skol Cup.

This period of Brian's life was certainly a hectic one. He was working in the Clydesdale Bank, as well as studying two evenings a week for the bank professional exams. In addition he was training two nights a week at Falkirk and playing on Saturdays.

It was also during this time that Brian made his commitment as a Christian: "I had a Christian back-ground and went to church but it didn't really mean anything. It was something that you did out of routine almost. After leaving school I drifted away. Then one day in the car on the way to football at Falkirk, we started talking about the purpose of life. One of the others said that Jesus was going to come back. After that game I went home and opened up the Bible and from then on the Bible became real. I realised that God loves me and that Jesus had died for me. That night was the turning point. That was the night I became a Christian.''

That year he was chosen to represent Scotland at semi-professional level in a tournament in Holland between England, Scotland, Holland and Italy. Brian played in two of the three games and Scotland won the tournament. This was not very significant in itself but it represented another step up the ladder to top-level football. At the end of the 1984–85 season, Brian had a talk with the Falkirk manager who told him that he thought he was good enough to play full-time professional football. Brian was excited by the prospect and waited to see if any clubs were interested in signing him.

There was an enquiry from Charlton Athletic and Brian went off to meet the Charlton manager, Lennie Lawrence. While waiting at the hotel for the meeting, he decided to ring Falkirk to tell the manager that he had arrived at the hotel. The Falkirk manager told him that Aberdeen were interested in him. Brian was delighted. If he could have chosen a club he wanted to play for, it would have been Aberdeen. So he signed for Aberdeen for £60,000, being incidentally one of the last players signed by Aberdeen's manager, Alex Ferguson, before his departure to become manager of Manchester United.

There was a certain irony in the timing. Brian had slogged away for three years at night school on his banking exams, spurred on by the knowledge that promotion to a higher level in the bank would follow. He sat and passed the exams in the summer of 1985. The next thing he did was to resign from the bank to become a full-time professional footballer.

Brian's progress at Aberdeen was steady rather than spectacular. Aberdeen already had in Willie Miller and Alex McLeish the two best central defenders in the country, each with over 60 Scottish caps. Inevitably his opportunities were limited. He made his debut for Aberdeen in the last game of the 1985–86 season, at Clydebank on 3rd May. Aberdeen won 6–0. That season Aberdeen won the Skol Cup and the Scottish Cup and finished fourth in the league. While Brian played only one game, it was still good to be part of such a successful club.

Over the next three seasons Brian played 20, 16 and 27 league games (out of 36). While he had not yet established himself as a first choice in the Aberdeen team, he was an accepted member of the first team squad, travelling to all the games, often being named as sub as well as coming into the team if any defender was injured.

During this period Aberdeen reached two Skol Cup finals and finished no lower than fourth in the Scottish Premier Division.

Ian Porterfield, who had succeeded Alex Ferguson as manager of Aberdeen, was certainly well pleased with Brian's progress. "He's grown in stature and is now a very important part of our squad. Alex McLeish and Willie Miller are having to play out of their skins to keep him out."

Brian's own assessment of his position at that time was: "I have often been asked how I coped with being on the fringe of the first team. The answer is that I got used to it but I never accepted it. Over the first four seasons at Aberdeen there was an improvement and each season I played more games. My faith helped me to have patience and to accept that there was a purpose and although it didn't happen as I might have wanted it, I knew that everything was in God's hands and God was in control."

Brian was single when he came to Aberdeen but not for long. One of his team-mates, Tommy McIntyre, had a girlfriend called Lindsay who worked at the airport. Lindsay had a friend called Donna. Knowing that Donna was a Christian, Lindsay told her that Aberdeen had a new player, called Brian Irvine, who was a Christian, too.

Donna said that she would be happy to take Brian to her church or introduce him to some of her Christian friends if he wanted. In the end Tommy and Lindsay arranged for Brian and Donna to meet on a blind date.

Looking back, Brian and Donna see God's hand in bringing them together. The timing could not have been better. In the previous year Donna had been at something of a crossroads in her life. She was a Christian but not fully committed. While she was going to church on Sundays, she was living life to the full the rest of the week, with little regard for God. But she had recently bought a flat in Aberdeen and the financial pressures involved were curtailing her social life. As a result she found herself getting more involved in the church than before. Shortly before meeting Brian she had recommitted her life to Christ and had decided to be baptised.

As their friendship grew, they both became more committed as Christians and have continued to support and encourage each other in the faith ever since. After nine months they were engaged and then married the next year.

Throughout their marriage Donna has supported Brian fully in the pressures of his life in football, although she is by no means a football fan and only watches him play occasionally. But her knowledge of football is increasing. As she says, "I now know that it is a goal when the ball goes into the net!"

Aberdeen reached the Skol Cup Final in 1988 and 1989. In 1988 Aberdeen lost 3–2 to Rangers, while in 1989 they beat Rangers 2–1. Both finals were played in front of over 70,000. Brian was one of the Aberdeen substitutes in both games. But the difference between the two finals was striking. He recalls, "In 1989, even though I only came on as a substitute late in the game it was great to be part of it, especially as it was my first winners' medal. I had played in the 1988 final when we lost. The difference between winning and losing is phenomenal. If you lose you go up and get your medal and then into the dressing room, get changed and it is just another game. The high of winning is fantastic. Being on the park when the final whistle blew was a great moment."

That the Skol Cup final is held on a Sunday led the *Sunday Post* to published an article on Brian under the heading "Aberdeen's holy warrior". The article quoted Brian's views on Sunday football: "Sunday is the Lord's day and I certainly wouldn't like to play every Sunday. I prefer to keep Sunday clear for worship but I have no problem making an exception on this occasion." The paper also reported that arrangements had been made for Brian to attend church prior to the game.

On one occasion on a pre-season tour to Holland, Brian had asked the manager if he could go to church on the Sunday morning. The manager said there would be no problem with that. Then he added, "There are a few of the other players who could do with going to church, do you think you could take them too!"

In November 1989 one of Aberdeen's regular central defenders, Willie Miller, sustained a serious injury which was to keep him out of action for five months. As always in the tough world of professional sport, one man's misfortune is another's opportunity. Brian Irvine played in every game for Aberdeen during that five-month period.

Aberdeen had already won the Skol Cup and were to finish second in the League behind Rangers who had led the table since before Christmas. The other competition was the Scottish Cup. Aberdeen progressed easily to the semi-final of the cup, with Brian playing in every game and even scoring in the 4–1 win over Hearts in the quarter-final.

In the semi-final Aberdeen beat Dundee United 4–0 with Brian scoring the first goal. Match reports also gave the second goal to Brian but he later pointed out that it had been put in by a Dundee United player and should therefore be recorded as an own goal. The press commended Brian for his honesty.

While Brian had already been part of two Skol Cup finals, the prospect of playing in the Scottish Cup Final was on a different level. For one thing, the Cup Final is the climax to the season, shown live on television. For another, Brian was to be in the starting line-up as opposed to just coming on as a substitute as in the Skol Cup finals.

The final was against Celtic. It was a game with nothing between the teams. While both had chances to win it there were no goals in the 90 minutes' play. Half-an-hour's extra time followed but also failed to produce any goals. This led to a situation which everyone had dreaded: the Scottish Cup was to be decided by a penalty shoot-out for the first time in its 116-year-history. Each team was to take five penalties.

Brian was quick to make his position clear. He did not want to be one of the players taking a penalty! But Brian was not to escape. Five Aberdeen players and five Celtic players took penalties. Four from each team scored. That made it 4–4. Now each team was to take a penalty in turn, with the first team which was ahead when an equal number of penalties had been taken winning the cup.

Four more players from each team took and scored penalties, making it 8–8. Now only two Aberdeen players had not taken a penalty – goalkeeper Theo Snelders and Brian. Celtic's Anton Rogan took his team's tenth penalty. It was saved by Snelders. Brian Irvine picked up the ball, placed it on the penalty spot and drove it past the Celtic goalkeeper, Pat Bonner. It was 9–8 and Aberdeen had won the cup!

Afterwards Brian said, "I was really nervous as I stepped up to take the kick but I just said a prayer and put my faith in God. The moment the ball hit the net was fantastic. It's a feeling I will never be able to describe." Later he told a newspaper, "It wasn't my strength, it was God's. If I took another penalty tomorrow, I would miss for I can't take penalties."

On the Monday after the game, the front page headline in the *Daily Record* was "God won me the Cup – exclusive by Don's hero Brian Irvine". While Brian was delighted that the article identified him as a Christian and gave the glory to God, he was a bit disappointed at the sensational headline.

The following year Brian was closer to the FA Cup than the Scottish Cup. He watched the FA Cup Final between Nottingham Forest and Tottenham Hotspur from a hospital bed in London, recovering from a minor operation to treat a niggling injury. He saw Paul Gascoigne carried from the field injured. A few hours later he discoverd that Gazza was in the same hospital, when the rest of the Spurs team turned up with the cup!

Another of the perks of playing for a successful club like Aberdeen was European football. Aberdeen had won the European Cup Winners' Cup in 1983, beating

Real Madrid in the final. Brian's first opportunity came in October 1986, away to Sion of Switzerland. Aberdeen lost 3–0 and were eliminated from the competition. It was, however, all valuable experience for Brian: "Even though we lost, I remember before the game thinking – I am playing in a European Cup game, this is every schoolboy's dream."

In the next two seasons there were further opportunies for Brian to sample European football. He played against Feyenoord and Rapid Vienna. Both times the ties were drawn with Aberdeen losing on the away-goals rule (i.e., in the event of a tie, goals scored away from home count double).

In 1990 Aberdeen defeated Salmina of Cyprus and then were drawn against Legia Warsaw of Poland. A few months prior to the game someone had given Brian a copy of the book *Goal Behind the Curtain* by Cliff Rennie (Christian Focus Publications 1990). The book tells the fictional story of a Christian footballer, Doug Mackay, who plays for the Scottish Premier League club, Dalkirk. In the UEFA Cup the team was drawn successively against teams from Czechoslovakia, Romania and Albania. Each time Doug is asked to take Bibles to Christians in the country where he is to play. With a few adventures, he succeeds.

An irony in the book is that one of the European ties is settled by the penalty shoot-out. Doug, who hates taking penalties, is the ninth player called upon. He scores the winning penalty. Now where else have we heard about a reluctant penalty-taker, scoring the winner late on in a penalty shoot-out?

Not only did Brian read the book, but when he went to speak at a church he met the author, Cliff Rennie. So when he flew to Warsaw with the Aberdeen squad, Brian was carrying not only a few Bibles in Polish and Russian but also a gift from his church to a church in Warsaw. The flight was delayed. This made Brian a little apprehensive about his meeting with the Polish Christian who was to collect the Bibles and the gift from him. But no sooner had he entered the hotel than a stranger walked up to him and asked, "Are you Brian Irvine?" Brian was delighted to hand over the gifts and to thank God for working everything out.

When Scotland manager, Andy Roxburgh, named his squad of players for the international against Romania in the European Championship on 12th September, 1990, it was of only academic interest to Brian. He glanced at it to see how many of his Aberdeen team-mates were included. The answer was three – Robert Connor, Stewart McKimmie and Alex McLeish.

By the Saturday before Wednesday's game, Roxburgh's squad was falling apart. When central defenders Craig Levein, David McPherson and Richard Cough all withdrew, it occurred to Brian that there were not many Scottish central defenders left! He wondered if he had a chance. He prayed about it with some Christian friends on the Saturday night, not asking that he would be selected but that God's will would be done and that he would be able to accept it whether selected or not.

On the Sunday morning Brian and Donna Irvine went off to the Deeside Christian Fellowship as usual. As they came into the house after the service, the telephone was ringing. He discovered that manager Alex Smith had been trying to contact him all morning. He told Brian that he had been called into the Scottish squad for the international and was to report to Hampden Park that afternoon. He later said that his first reaction had been panic. He hurriedly packed his kit and set off on the four-hour drive to Glasgow.

It was only as he neared Glasgow that Brian realised

that he did not have a clue how to find Hampden. While he had played there a few times, he had always travelled on the team coach. He had to stop and ask for directions three times before finding it, prompting the headline in the *Aberdeen Press and Journal*: "Scotland new boy Irvine loses way to Hampden". Another paper picked up the point that he had been at church when the SFA had been trying to contact him.

Brian's reaction to his call-up was typically modest: "It is everyone's dream to play for their country and I am no different . . . I'm realistic enough to see that I am not here as a first or even a second choice. I only made it because of the injuries but that doesn't make it any less enjoyable."

At first he felt a little over-awed by being there. Having three Aberdeen team-mates in the squad was a great help, and soon he was made to feel entirely at home. Manager Andy Roxburgh indicated to the press on the Sunday "the distinct possibility that he would play", adding that he had been impressed with his club form and how well he and Alex McLeish combined together. When the Scotland team was announced, Brian was in it.

When I spoke to him on the telephone at lunch-time on the day of the match, he was excited yet hardly believing that it was all happening. When I told him that I was flying up just to see him play, he remarked that it meant a lot to him that so many friends had spoken to him and were sharing his big day.

With the birth of the baby imminent, Donna travelled with a friend to the game – under strict instructions from her doctor not to get too excited! Donna was probably the calmest person around. So much so, in fact, that Brian remarked to her during the week after the game, "If it had been me, I would have had the baby long ago with all the excitement." The game itself was an unforgettable experience.

The build-up to the game was the one thing that Brian found hard to handle. Arriving at Hampden early, the players had a look at the pitch, a long warm-up, TV interviews – it all dragged on. Then when the time came for the players to go on to the pitch, there were still the national anthems. While standing there in his Scottish international shirt was one of the proudest moments of his life, he just wanted to get on with the game.

The attendance at the game was only 12,081 as the game was being screened on live television. Chants of "If you hate the telly clap your hands" echoed round the ground. But Brian was enjoying it all too much to notice the size of the crowd.

In the early stages of the game the Romanians, displaying great skill, threatened to overrun Scotland. Romania took the lead in the nineteenth minute. John Robertson equalised after 37 minutes and then Ally McCoist scored after 75 minutes to set up a 2–1 win for Scotland. The *Daily Record* summed up the performance: "Scotland have fielded better teams but none in recent time who tried so hard."

The papers were generally satisfied with Brian's performance. The *Record*'s assessment was: "Nervous at the start but settled to give a promising show on his debut. Covered intelligently throughout." The *Sun* reported: "New boy Irvine slotted in like a veteran."

The month of September was extremely busy for Brian. In addition to the international and the usual Saturday games, there was a European game in Cyprus and a Skol Cup semi-final with Rangers. This all caused Donna a few problems as she and Brian were determined that he would be present at the birth. Baby Hannah Irvine waited until all the important game were past and put in her appearance on Tuesday, 25th September, with Brian in attendance.

During that month Brian was using the same Bible Study guide that he had used the previous year. He was interested to compare some of the comments that he had written the previous year with his present feelings. In 1988 he had written, "Feeling very low about football," at a time when he was out of the team. A year later he had a Scottish Cup Winner's Medal, a Skol Cup Winner's medal, a Scottish Cap – not to mention a baby!

Brian was retained in the Scottish squad for the next international (against Switzerland in October 1990). Although with everyone fit again he did not play, it was encouraging that the manager had felt he had done enough against Romania to be retained in the squad.

Before the squad was picked for the trip to Bulgaria in November, manager Andy Roxburgh rang Brian to say that he was leaving him out. He commented that he saw no point in taking him to Sofia without any prospect of playing. That the manager should take the trouble to telephone, rather than leaving him to find out from the newspapers that he had been omitted from the squad, was a gesture that Brian appreciated. In the event, when the squad was hit by injuries, Roxburgh contacted Aberdeen with a view to calling Brian in as cover. As he was carrying an injury, however, he could not go.

Brian almost completed his set of Scottish medals in 1991 when Aberdeen finished second in the league. At one stage they trailed Rangers by 8 points but closed the gap to set up a climax on the last day of the season when Aberdeen met Rangers needing only a draw to clinch the title. However, Rangers won 2–0 and became champions.

As a big defender – 6 foot 2 inches and 13 stones – whose job is to stop the opposition from scoring, Brian has no qualms about tackling hard but does not deliberately commit fouls. He has never been sent off and only rarely been cautioned by the referee.

He feels that the desire to retaliate when you yourself are fouled is probably the most difficult thing to cope with. "In your own strength and feelings you would but prayer helps and in God's strength you can handle the situation. I remember an incident in a big game against Rangers. I committed a foul. The player I had fouled got up and pushed me to the ground. I jumped up immediately, thought about having a go at him but was able to walk away. A number of people spoke to me about that and I was pleased to have had that opportunity to express my faith on the pitch. But it isn't always easy."

Brian does not see "religion" and "football" as different compartments of his life, but as two parts of an integrated whole. As he puts it, "It is not just a case of going to church on Sunday, it is the way you live your life the rest of the week – including football." With that attitude it is as natural for Brian to pray about football as about anything else. "I always pray before a game because it is part of my life. I do not pray that Aberdeen will win but that I will play the game fairly and that the outcome will be what is meant to happen."

One of the secrets of Brian's and Donna's attitude to life is their involvement in the Deeside Christian Fellowship at Milltimber on the outskirts of Aberdeen. "We have received a lot of encouragement there. The fellowship is fantastic; there is great unity. We are really learning a lot there. It has been a great help in my football. The church prays for me and supports me and a block of church members have season tickets and that is a great encouragement to me. As well as that I am an officer in the 1st Kintore Company of the Boys' Brigade. I find that a good form of service. Being in the BB was a big influence in my life and I am glad of the chance to put something back into it."

In 1990 the 11th Airdrie Company camped near Aberdeen and it was a great delight for Brian to be able to see his old friend Jim McKerley again and to be able to show him and the boys around Aberdeen's Pittodrie Stadium. The timing of their visit was excellent as the Skol Cup and the Scottish Cup were in Aberdeen's possession and on display.

Brian Irvine is not what anyone would call a superstar of football. He is rather an honest professional who has worked hard to make the best of his talents. Throughout his career – without preaching at anyone – he has always been ready to take a stand for what he believes in.

While most observers would feel that Brian still has a long way to go in the game, he is unlikely to have many years with as much excitement as 1990.

CAREER SUMMARY

League appearances

Falkirk	1984–84	38
Aberdeen	1985–90	95

Transfers
June 1985   Falkirk to Aberdeen – £60,000

International appearances
Scotland v Romania   September 1990 (European
Championship)

Honours
1989   Skol Cup Runner-Up
1990   Scottish Cup Winner's Medal
        Skol Cup Winner's Medal

ALAN KNOTT

Most people have memories of curling up in front of a fire on a winter's evening, opening the family photo album and remembering a much enjoyed holiday.

"There's Aunt Agnes fast asleep on the beach after a big lunch – she was a character!"

"Oh look! That couple we met in Spain when our car broke down – they took us to that awful bar – the music was so loud."

"Do you remember when the tent collapsed with the kids inside it?"

And so it goes on – happy memories.

Recalling the career of Alan Knott is rather like remembering a favourite holiday. He played cricket for Kent more or less continually from 1964 to 1985. During that time he kept wicket for England on 95 occasions. It would have been 100 if the five he played against the Rest of the World XI in 1970 had counted. His final tally of victims was an amazing 269 (250 catches and 19 stumpings). He scored 4,389 Test runs including 5 hundreds and 30 scores of over fifty, at an average of 32.75 per innings. He was one of the first recruits to Kerry Packer's world series cricket in 1977. He offended the cricketing establishment still further by joining the 1981 "rebel" tour to South Africa. His career is a catalogue of success and controversy.

And yet you will not find anyone with a bad word to say about him in professional cricket; he is universally admired as a man, and as a professional cricketer. Many have smiled at his idiosyncracies, wondered at his outrageous batting improvisations and admired the speed and dexterity of his catching. Yet he remains an essentially private man. His Christian faith and his commitment to his family have long been higher priorities than his career, and have dictated certain controversial decisions he has made.

It would be impossible to do justice to so long, varied and successful a career in one short chapter. So what we will do is look back at eight "snapshots" of Alan's life. We will see him as a child, as a batsman, as a wicketkeeper, as a seeker after God, as a so-called mercenary, as a husband and father and as an adviser, coach and elder statesman in cricket which he is today. Some of the pictures we look at will be personal, some even intimate. Hopefully, by the time we close the "album" we will feel we know the man who is acknowledged as one of the really great post-war English cricketers.

Snapshot 1: The Boy

Our first picture is of a small six-year-old. He is standing beside the goal posts on a largely deserted football field at Belvedere in Kent. Between the "sticks" is a stocky, curly-haired man with a determined look on his face. The boy is the young Alan Knott and the goalkeeper is his Dad, Eric.

Alan's early life was dominated by sport. His father kept wicket for Erith Technical College Association and goal for Erith Council. Most Saturday afternoons were spent at one sports ground or another. He remembers distracting his father one afternoon and nearly costing the team a match. It was just before kick-off and after the toss the Erith goalkeeper had to walk the length of the field to take up his station.

The young Alan dawdled his way around the touchline, dribbling the ever present soccer ball and was still on his way when the opposition kicked off. Eric, distracted by his son some way away, did not notice the speculative shot by the inside forward who lobbed the ball over Eric's head for a very soft goal.

Alan's competitive instincts were honed in those early years. His father was a fine keeper who set himself and his talented younger son very high standards. He always hoped Alan would go into professional sport. For a number of years football seemed the most likely route he would follow. The family were great Charlton Athletic supporters, although it was eventually to Crystal Palace Football Club that Alan went for trials. He heard nothing back, and so cricket became the focus of his attention.

At Belmont Primary School and later at Northumberland Heath Secondary Modern School, near Erith, the young Knott excelled as a bowler. Indeed, when he eventually signed professionally for Kent in 1962 it was as an off-spin bowler and opening batsman. He did keep wicket as well but he recalls the advice of Leslie Ames, perhaps the greatest wicketkeeper batsman of all time and a predecessor of Knott's behind the stumps at Kent: "Concentrate on your bowling, son."

Academic attainment never figured highly, although he managed three "O" levels. Even as a child his mind was quick and agile, like his movements. He was capable of long periods of concentration which served him well all through his career. He has an inventive mind, and in retirement is regularly sought out by professional cricketers to analyse technique and discuss new ways of coping with the modern game. His teachers identified this ability early and he was encouraged to consider a career in teaching. It is interesting to note that in retirement from his playing career his chief pleasure is derived from coaching others.

From a very early age he concentrated his mind on becoming excellent in his sport. It was what he wanted out of life and it was what his parents wanted for him. His whole life has been lived within the environment of sport – clubhouses, pavilions, practice areas, changing rooms. This is his natural habitat, and it is where he is most relaxed and comfortable. Many a youngster has sat at his feet in the changing room just as he did at his father's, long after everyone else has gone home, and drawn out great wisdom on the game from one of its masters.

Religion played a small part in his upbringing. His mother was a Roman Catholic with a firm faith, but she "lapsed" after her marriage. Sport was the main "religion" in the family, and it was practised faithfully. Yet the seeds of later Christian faith were sown in those early years. Alan suffered terribly from nightmares and was often tossing and turning through the night. He attended a school Christmas carol service and heard the teachers ending prayers with the words "through Jesus Christ our Lord". Lying awake in his bed, fearful of the dreams to come, young Alan began to pray. He would always end with that same formula, "through Jesus Christ our Lord". The nightmares ended, and typically of Alan he has never abandoned his habit of praying at night.

Snapshot 2: The Batsman 1

We are catapulted into the cauldron of Test cricket in Georgetown, Guyana against the West Indies. It is the final Test of the 1967–68 series against Gary Sobers's West Indian team. Alan's county captain, Colin Cowdrey, had led his England team to a great victory in the fourth Test following Sobers's controversially generous declaration. In Georgetown England needed 307 to win. Our snapshot shows Jeff Jones, England's number 11 and a ferret (so bad a batsman that he comes in after the rabbits) edging a ball from off-spinner Lance Gibbs to third man. Alan, at the non-striker's end, is 70 not out, and has been batting for over four hours. Both batsmen have one hand in the air and are clearly saying "no".

It was a very dramatic moment, and a great memory for Alan. ". . . In only my fourth Test Match I was able to help England draw a match which enabled us to win the series." The television commentator on the famous scene was Dennis Compton. He was unable to understand why they did not run so that Knott would face the last two balls. "Why don't they run? Why don't they run?" he shouts into the microphone. This was before the bowling of a mandatory 20 overs in the final hour of a match, and from where he was sitting Compton could see that Gibb's over would be the last of the game. Out in the middle it looked different. Alan was convinced that there would be one more over, and he and Jeff Jones had concluded that the tailender would have terrible problems with Sobers's left arm googlies and chinamen. Much better, they thought, for Jones to keep Gibbs out and leave Sobers to Knott. Jones survived those next two balls, the umpires removed the bails, the match was saved and the series won.

It had taken him only a season and a half to establish himself as Kent's 1st XI wicketkeeper. When he arrived in 1962 Tony Catt was the no. 1 keeper and Derek Ufton the no. 2. They were both very fine players but it was, nonetheless, an unusual thing in Kent to have no truly world class keeper. For years first Leslie Ames and then the ebullient, extrovert Godfrey Evans had kept wicket for both Kent and England. By the end of the 1964 season

Catt had retired and Ufton had become manager of Plymouth Argyle Football Club. At the tender age of 18 Alan took up the mantle of his two great predecessors. Over the next two decades he certainly equalled, and many would say exceeded, all that they achieved.

His first Test Match was against Pakistan in 1967 and he began by taking seven catches. He also began a practice that he never abandoned for the next 94 games. He began the day by drinking two teaspoonfuls of kaolin morphine: "It really does relax you and calm the butterflies." It is interesting to note that in the drugs-conscious 'nineties a Test cricketer would not be permitted this help!

In those early years Knott came to see that his batting was going to be of immense importance if he was to succeed as an international cricketer. Jim Parks was in the England side, and though a fine wicketkeeper, his batting had secured him selection. On tour in the West Indies, Parks was selected for the England team for the first three Tests but batted poorly and this gave Alan his chance. He made a 50 in the Fourth Test at Trinidad as England won, and then the epic 70 at Georgetown to save the game and the series.

From then until he signed for World Series cricket in 1977 Alan was England's first and automatic choice for wicketkeeper.

Snapshot 3: The Wicketkeeper

It is August 1971 and Knott is playing for England at the Oval against India. The batsman is the Indian right-hander Sardesai who has 40 not out to his name. The left-arm slow bowler is Knott's Kent and England colleague Derek Underwood. The ball turns quite sharply and Sardesai gets a thick outside edge. The picture shows Knott moving a long way to his right and catching the ball in one hand almost level with the stumps. It was a fantastic catch, and is regarded by Alan as the best he ever took.

This "snap" evokes all kinds of memories. Between 1968 and 1971 Knott was at his peak as a keeper. He is quite clear in his own mind that he excelled standing up in 1969. An injury in his lower back caused a slight adjustment in his technique in 1970. It is typical of him that his recollection of these things is so detailed. His speed, agility and reflexes were second to none at this time. The Sardesai catch was a great catch but it was one of many. But the picture also reminds us of one of the great combinations in English post-war cricket – Knott and Underwood. They broke into the Kent and England sides at about the same time and developed an uncanny understanding which accounted for numerous batsmen over the years. At one stage Knott would signal to Underwood if he thought he should bowl a slower ball by raising his head a few inches as the bowler ran in. One day, while practising in the nets, Alan started calling out what type of ball he thought Derek was going to bowl – "arm ball", "slower one", "quicker and shorter", etc. So disturbed by this was Derek, realising that if Alan could "work him out" it would not be long before County and Test batsmen did too, so he adjusted his run up. Instead of coming in in full view of the batsman he developed a technique of running in behind the umpire, so that the batsman's view was obscured. It is a typical example of their co-operation and inventiveness. They were a formidable team.

Underwood's assessment of Knott is therefore worth listening to. He is quoted at length by David Lemon in his portrait of Knott in *Ten Great Wicketkeepers* (Stanley Paul) : "Day in and day out he is the best in the world. No one gives himself so totally to the game. As soon as we arrive at the ground he is changed and ready to practise. We have to bowl to him to get his rhythm going and then he wants balls thrown to left and right so that he can practise diving, gently at first and then with increasing difficulty. As soon as the skipper has tossed up it is more practice, further wicketkeeping routines, or if we are batting, he is round to the nets and practising in earnest. It doesn't matter whether we are playing at Ashby de la Zouch or Lords, the routine is the same – total dedication."

Years later at a Christians in Sport dinner at Luton Town Football Club I asked him what advice he would give a youngster going into professional sport. His reply was simple: "Never stop trying."

In his autobiography, *It's Knott Cricket* (Macmillan), there is a side-on photograph of the Underwood action. The caption reads, "Part of the perfect Derek Underwood action . . . thanks Deadly." Many people think of Knott as a specialist at standing back. Certainly against the medium pacers, like Bob Woolmer and John Shepherd, he defied the advice of many pundits who wanted to see him up at the stumps in the manner of Ames and Evans, and indeed his contemporary Bob Taylor. Alan argued that top class batsmen strayed from the crease much less than club players, and therefore stumping opportunities off the medium pacers would be very few. He believed that by standing back he was able to catch more of the thick edges which would have been very hard chances standing up. Having said that, his keeping over the years to Underwood, who had prodigious powers of lift and turn especially on helpful pitches, and bowled at a lively pace, and to whom he always stood up, of course, was outstandingly brilliant.

Broadcaster Brian Johnson tells a lovely story. "Johnners" was a great advocate of "standing up" and was frustrated by Knott's preference for going back for the medium pacers. When Alan approached him to write an article for this benefit brochure Johnston said he would, but only on the condition that he was paid a fee. Alan was taken aback – normally people contributed for nothing. "Johnners" replied that his fee would be that Knott would stand up to Woolmer in a Test Match the following summer. Sure enough in the Oval Test of 1976 against the West Indies, Woolmer came on to bowl. Knott immediately came up to the stumps, looked up at the commentary box in the pavilion and gave the thumbs up sign. Mind you, after one over, he went back again!

Snapshot 4: The Husband and Father

Now this one is a bit of a scoop. Our hero is photographed early one morning, before anyone else is about, sneaking back into the England team hotel in Adelaide during the 1974–75 tour of Australia. What, you might say, is this doing in a Christian book?

To get to the bottom of this mystery it is necessary to go back to 21st March, 1969, and the occasion of Alan's marriage to Jan. They had met in 1965 when Alan was working for Associated Portland Cement Manufacturers in Northfleet. Jan's job was as an assistant secretary and one of her first jobs was to send Alan's wages to his parents' house because he was away on a four-weeks Cavaliers tour of the West Indies.

The first major tour overseas after their marriage was to Australia under Ray Illingworth's captaincy in 1970–71. It was a wonderful tour, culminating in the winning of the Ashes in Sydney. Alan always rated Illingworth the best captain he ever played under, and many commentators would say that this was his best tour as a keeper.

But it was spoiled for him by Jan's absence. She stayed at home for the whole six months. Afterwards they vowed never to be apart for so long again. The previous winter they had been together in Tasmania where Alan had had a coaching job. In 1971–72, there being no MCC tour, they had a rare winter together at home and made a brief holiday trip to California. During the 73–74 tour to the West Indies Jan had enjoyed her time with the team very much, despite the difficulties of fitting in the trip to the Caribbean at the same time as she was establishing their own sports business in Herne Bay.

The decision of the authorities to permit wives to stay only 21 nights with their husbands during the 74–75 MCC tour to Australia, coupled with the ludicrous ruling that they must travel on different flights, was probably the main reason why Alan played 95 times for England rather than 195. In fact, after the centenary Test in 1977 Alan was told that the regulations concerning wives were going to be even tighter on forthcoming tours, and children would not be permitted to come at all.

In his autobiography Alan describes what he was forced to do. "We were living in adjacent hotels. You can guess where I was every night – in the hotel next door, and rushing back in the morning to have breakfast in my own hotel." Alan accepts that he had particularly strong views on this subject. For years he had argued that the system helped to break up marriages by forcing people apart. The husband was travelling the world, meeting new people and experiencing different cultures which the wife was denied. When she did appear on tour all the arrangements for accommodation and travel had to be made by the player himself. This was a job most of them could do without amidst the pressure of an Ashes series. So for both moral and pragmatic reasons the rules made no sense. The management argued that wives and children undermined team spirit, and that it was unfair on players who could not afford to have their wives with them. Alan felt, and he still does, that married couples should be together, and he laughs at suggestions that the presence of wives on that tour affected the players' form: "As I recall, it was Dennis Lillee and Jeff Thomson who affected our form."

How different it all was when he joined World Series cricket in 1977. By this time James, Alan's and Jan's only child, had arrived and was three. The previous winter he had stayed in England when Alan toured India, Jan joining him for a month half-way through the tour. On his return the family-minded Knott was horrified to find that James hardly recognised him. As by now they were Christians, Alan and Jan prayed about what they should do about subsequent tours. While they were praying the phone rang: it was Tony Greig inviting Alan to join Kerry Packer's "circus".

The offer was three winters' cricket in Australia with no restriction on the presence of wives and families. Arrangements were made for the families at every ground and hotel and Jan and James were welcome to fly and stay with Alan whenever they wanted. As far as they are concerned, "that telephone call from Tony Greig was a wonderful answer to prayer."

Alan Knott never went on tour with England again.

Snapshot 5: "The Seeker After God"
This is another very personal, almost intimate, photograph of Alan and Jan. The picture shows them sitting in a small room. With them is the Pastor of the Kensington Temple in London and his wife. They are sitting around a table with their hands clasped, obviously praying. It is 1974.

For a number of years Alan and Jan had enjoyed a friendship with a Christian family from America, the Severns. "Doc" Severn had advised Alan in the past on diet and fitness. They had spent time with them in California and met up regularly in England. Alan recalls Billy Severn, Doc's son, who was a pastor, bowling at the England players in the nets at the Oval. Unfortunately he slipped and covered his smart trousers with mud and grass stains – to everyone's amusement. Typically, Billy carried on as if nothing had happened.

As a family the Severns demonstrated the difference Christ makes to a family. They prayed together, and not just before meals. They attended church regularly. They spoke freely and openly about Jesus, about His reality in their lives and the truth of His life, death and resurrection. In the autumn of 1973 they prayed with Alan and Jan in California that the Lord would come into their lives. Until this point Alan had always concentrated on giving reasons for not believing in God. Billy suggested that he be more positive, looking for reasons *for* believing in God. He challenged Alan to start living as if he believed in God and advised him to use the long journeys which all professional cricketers have to make to think and pray about becoming a Christian.

The following summer the Knotts experienced two remarkable answers to their prayers . . . and then a third. First, Jan's brother survived a severe car crash against all predictions. As Alan and Jan drove from Herne Bay to Aberystwyth to see him they prayed for his recovery. On arrival Alan felt sure Brian would be all right despite the medical prognosis of possible death, or at least brain damage. Within six weeks he had left hospital and quickly made a remarkable recovery.

Next they received news that a possible court case involving the *Sunday Express* had been dropped. This had been a great cause of anxiety for Alan. It had all begun during the 1970–71 tour of Australia when Dennis Compton wrote an article suggesting that Illingworth and Knott were "cheating" people out. The players' financial backer had pulled out and Alan was looking at possible legal fees of £40,000 – a vast sum of money for him. Out of the blue he heard that the *Sunday Express* had agreed to settle out of court.

The third answer came in that little room at Kensington Temple. Some time earlier the Severns had introduced Alan and Jan to Eldin Corsie who was then the Pastor. They had become friends and occasionally Alan and Jan would attend church. Alan was beginning to realise the importance of Jesus Christ in his life and knew that the time had come to make a commitment. So at the end of a service one Sunday he and Jan answered the call to come forward during the singing of a hymn and give their lives to the Lord. In the small room they confided to the Pastor that they had been trying for a baby for several years but without success. They felt very disappointed. So they all prayed about it. Not long after, in fact just after Alan had arrived in Australia for the 74–75 tour, Jan rang to say she was pregnant.

Becoming a Christian had been a gradual process for Alan, as it is for most people. His intellectual objections had disappeared. The process reached the natural, or perhaps supernatural, climax at church that day. He had known for some time that he would be making the decision to become a Christian. His actual moment of commitment came when the news of the court case came through. He was very aware of someone looking after them. By going forward at church that day he publicly demonstrated what he had privately decided. Alan and Jan have a time they can look back to, and know that they made up their own minds.

Alan's relationship with the Lord is very real and meaningful to him. I recall walking down the King's Road in London with him and listening as he quite naturally began to talk to Jesus. On another occasion we were having lunch together and he said grace: "Hello, Jesus, just a word to say thank you for the food." His faith is in sharp contrast to the formal "religious" forms that are practised in many churches, but it is all the more real for that.

Snapshot 6: The Batsman 2

We are transported forward in time and northwards in direction. It is 1976 and the scene is the Fourth Test at Headingley against the West Indies. England are in trouble at 169 for 5 when Alan Knott joins his captain Tony Greig at the crease. Our picture shows the giant Greig and the diminutive Knott deep in conversation in the middle of the wicket.

By 1976 Knott's Test career was nearing its end. This game at Leeds was his 77th. In the next Test at the Oval he took the world record number of dismissals for a wicketkeeper when he stumped Laurence Rowe off Underwood. In fact he scored his highest Test Score, 135, the following summer at Trent Bridge against the Australians.

But this partnership with Greig at Headingley was momentous. In 1976 West Indies were a great side. Their fast bowlers, Roberts, Holding, Daniel and Holder, were truly formidable. Viv Richards, Gordon Greenidge, Clive Lloyd, Alvin Kallicharran and Laurence Rowe were all world class batsmen. Bernard Julien, Knott's Kent colleague, was a genuine Test all-rounder. The first Test was a draw, with Alan playing despite a painful broken finger. The Lords Test was also drawn, but England lost the third match of the series at Old Trafford – they were bowled out on a difficult wicket for 71 and 126. Rumours that changes in the team were imminent were rife; in particular the press were calling for the heads of captain Greig and his first lieutenant wicketkeeper Knott.

It was a situation tailor-made for the batting of Knott. Time and again he got runs when England were deep in trouble. On this occasion both players made exactly 116. Watching the video of that great partnership gives a great deal of insight into the secret of Knott's success. His face is set in concentration for every ball. The grip of the bat with the top hand turned around and the chest opened up to the bowler is much in evidence. The often outrageously unorthodox shots are followed by a smile and a word with Greig. He is obviously trying like mad and loving every minute of it.

His batting style can also be seen in old film of him playing the Indian spinners in 1971. Venkataraghavan, Bedi and Chandrasekhar made as good a spin attack as there has been. Alan's nimble footwork, quick eye and audacious stoke play enabled him to attack them when others were mesmerised. Of course, as a wicketkeeper he was well able to read "spinners" and this gave him an advantage, but his method of playing the ball on the half volley, and if necessary, sweeping or pulling against the spin, resulted in some spectacular strokeplay. There will be few followers of English cricket in the 'seventies who have not been rendered speechless by some of Knott's amazing batting.

Snapshot 7: "The Mercenary"

The photogaph shows Alan Knott eating a meal in a restaurant in Durban, South Africa. He is being asked for his autograph by an Indian waiter. It is spring 1982.

Knott visited South Africa three times during his long career. The first two passed off relatively quietly – he competed in double wicket tournaments in 1972 and 1974–75 before going to Australia. They were both fleeting visits and only involved going to Johannesburg. His third visit with the South African Breweries "rebel" team caused bitterness, recrimination, and a three-year ban from Test cricket which ended his international career.

Plans had been brewing (excuse the pun) for some time. All county players received letters from the Test and County Cricket Board and their County clubs containing a mild warning of the consequences of going to play in South Africa for any kind of representative team. The England team were in India and Sri Lanka without Knott, who had opted out of overseas tours by this time even though he had been recalled to the England team during the astonishing 1981 series against Australia. He had in fact played his 95th and last Test at the Oval scoring a match-saving 70 not out in the second innings.

Some time after Christmas Alan was recruited for the month-long tour and, very importantly, he was permitted to take Jan and James with him. Uncertainty and an element of conspiracy surrounded all the preparations. "I prayed about it a lot," says Alan. "The Lord knew I wanted to go and that I thought it was right for me to do so. I prayed that if it was not right He would prevent me from going, or that if it was not right for the team to go ahead, He would stop it from taking place."

The outcry against the tour exceeded all the players' expectations. Alan is convinced that the cricket authorities in England privately hoped that the tour would go ahead. He thinks they wanted South Africa readmitted to international cricket. In South Africa they were greeted as heroes, but in the British media they were portrayed as villains. The cricketing establishment turned against them when they discovered the extent of the opposition to the tour in the black countries. Alan and his fellow players were genuinely shocked by the actions taken against them. He had always had good friends with South African connections. His hero at Kent had been Stuart Leary, a white South African. A great friend in the Kent team was Bob Woolmer, whose wife Gill is a South African. He had enjoyed a close relationship in the England side with Tony Greig, who had grown up in South Africa. He also argued that sport breaks down barriers, and it is always better to maintain contact.

The incident in the Durban restaurant is a case in point. The waiter was obviously a cricket enthusiast. Alan engaged him in conversation about cricket and mentioned that as an Indian he must be very proud of Sunil Gavaskar, the diminutive Indian Test opener who has scored more Test runs than any other player. To Alan's amazement, the waiter had never heard of him! "Surely," says Alan, "we did good in demonstrating and explaining to them that black and coloured cricketers elsewhere in the world were not only equal to but often better than whites."

Alan is clear in his condemnation of apartheid – there is very little racial prejudice in first class cricket simply because the players all know and respect each other so much. He feels that tours should have been encouraged. "Being a Christian," he writes, "I cannot imagine a missionary saying, 'We won't go there until apartheid is finished.'"

It is an illuminating comment. Knott cannot divorce his Christian faith from any part of his life. His relationship with his "greatest friend", Jesus, dominates all of his thinking. He sees himself as a Christian, first and foremost, in every situation. He is not a tub-thumping evangelist, but he is always unashamed to defend what he believes. His decision to tour South Africa has been condemned by many people, and undoubtedly the players themselves were surprised by the furore it caused and by the three-year ban which followed. We may disagree with Knott's decision to go, but we should resist the temptation to caricature all the "rebels" as closet racists. Alan thought and prayed long and hard about going. He really believes that from Christian, sporting and political perpectives the tour did more good than harm. Disagree with him if you must, but do not question his integrity.

Snapshot 8: "The Elder Statesman"

My final "snap" is a personal one. I have spent many delightful hours with Alan at cricket matches. I recall being in the changing-room at Worcester when he called out to one of the Kent players, "Hey, xxxx, you've got a problem with pornography. Come and talk to Andrew!" Only later, after he had shown me his pictures, did the very embarrassed player discover I was a clergyman.

On another occasion at Lords he woke up one of his colleagues with the words, "Wake up! God's been trying to get through to you for years; Andrew can tell you about Him."

When my team, Dorset, played Kent in the Nat West Cup at Canterbury in 1989, Alan, now retired from playing, took the trouble to come in to the changing-room and spend some time with the Dorset team. They, of course, were thrilled to see him, and enthralled by his knowledge of the game.

But the snapshot I have chosen is of Alan Knott, the England scout. Since retiring he has been employed by The Test and County Cricket Board as one of their regional talent spotters. This involves watching players and reporting on them to the England manager and selectors. He takes it very seriously indeed. Our photograph shows him seated in the top tier of the Lords pavilion, immediately behind the bowler's arm. It is cold up there so he is huddled in a blue anorak. He watches every ball intently and occasionally jots down something. On his lap is a tupperware box containing his lunch – which, as I look in, appears to be mainly nuts and raisins. He is a fastidious man about most things and extremely careful with his diet.

This picture shows a lot about Alan. He has always taken great care of his physical condition. The stretching exercises for which he became notorious were a deliberate strategy for keeping as loose and athletic as possible. After 1971 he found himself losing mobility and has had to work hard to maintain his form. Every day he does half an hour's stretching exercises as soon as he wakes up. Often he will listen to a tape of Bible readings or Christian music while he does it.

He is a great enthusiast for cricket. He loves to study the finer details of the game. In the early days he enjoyed long conversations with his Kent captain, Colin Cowdrey, who had an almost obsessive passion for discussing players' techniques. Watching players he will spot strengths and weaknesses which elude the less knowledgeable. He is constantly in demand. As Trevor Bailey once wrote of him, "He has probably forgotten more about first class cricket than many of our county coaches have ever known."

He carries within him certain apparent contradictions. He is a deeply committed Christian but finds church difficult. He loves the company of cricketers but is essentially a private man. He says he always "walked" (i.e. gave himself out if he edged a catch to the wicketkeeper) in county cricket, but rarely in Test cricket. He says, "I never intended to walk in Tests but sometimes did by mistake" – heading for the pavilion instinctively afte edging a ball to the wicketkeeper. He is tremendously perceptive about an individual's technical weaknesses, but when talking about players makes even a run-of-the-mill county pro sound like a world beater.

Yet all these strands in Alan seem quite consistent and reasonable. For all his "little ways" he is a very rounded, whole person. Central to this is the Christian faith which radiates out of his personality. He is in every sense a man of cricket and a man of God.

I leave the last word to Ivo Tennant, the cricket journalist, who wrote of him in *The Times* on the occasion of his retirement from the game in 1985: "He was quirky, faddy, conscientious, courteous, generous, as introverted off the field as he was extroverted on it. He played for the team and always tried. Kent and England do not know how lucky they were. Others had their peers, but above Knott was only the sky."

CAREER SUMMARY

Batting

	Innings	Not Out	Runs	Highest Score	Average
Tests	149	15	4,389	135	32.75
Other 1st Class	596	119	13,716	156	28.76
One-Day Internationals	14	4	200	50	20.00
Sunday League	127	27	1,628	60	16.28
Gillette/NatWest Cup	36	5	455	46	14.68
Benson & Hedges Cup	58	7	888	65	17.41

Test Hundreds
101 v New Zealand in 1971 at Auckland
116 v Pakistan   in 1971 at Edgbaston
106 v Australia   in 1975 at Adelaide
116 v West Indies   in 1976 at Headingley
135 v Australia   in 1977 at Trent Bridge

Highest First Class Score
156 v South Zone in 1972–73 at Bangalore

Wicketkeeping

	Catches	Stumpings
Tests	250	19
Other 1st Class	961	114
One-Day Internationals	15	1
Sunday League	183	35
Gillette/NatWest Cup	56	6
Benson & Hedges Cup	78	10

Bowling

Tests	None				
	Overs	Maidens	Runs	Wickets	Average
Other 1st Class	142	0	87	2	43.50

BERNHARD LANGER

The most amazing thing about Bernhard Langer's golf career is that it ever got started. Growing up in Anhausen near Augsburg in southern Germany was far from the ideal way to start on a career in professional golf.

Anhausen, a village of 1,200 people, was where his father, Erwin, had settled after fleeing as a refugee from Sudetenland in Czechoslovakia. When Hitler annexed Czechoslovakia in 1938 Erwin Langer had been forced to join the German army. At one stage, as a member of the defeated German army, he was put on a train bound for Russia but jumped off with Russian soldiers shooting at him. He escaped, walked all the way to Germany and became a bricklayer in Anhausen. All this seems another world now that the Berlin wall has come down and the two Germanies are united.

When Bernhard was growing up, golf in Germany was very much a minority sport, practised only by the rich élite. Bernhard's introduction to golf came through caddying at the nearby Augsburg Golf and Country Club. His older brother and sister found caddying a useful way of earning some pocket-money and at the tender age of eight and a half, Bernhard persuaded his parents to let him offer his services as a trolley-puller. The going rate was DM2.50 for nine holes! Eventually there was Bernhard's brother, his sister and about 10 of their friends from Anhausen who were caddying regularly at the club.

Being a caddy gave Bernhard his first opportunity to play the game. The caddies had a collection of clubs which had been discarded by the club members. While they were not allowed to play on the course until they were deemed to be able to play to a certain standard, they were allowed to develop their game on the club's practice range when it was not busy. It was there that Bernhard hit his first golf shots. In fact, he recalls spending hours hitting shots on that practice ground, a habit that would help him greatly in the future.

Some three months after he first went to the club, still two months short of his ninth birthday, he felt ready to ask the professional to have a look at him hitting some balls with a view to deciding if he had reached the standard which would permit him to play on the course. The professional watched him hit about 10 balls and then concluded that Bernhard looked as if he would not do too much damage to the course. He was allowed to play. From then on he started to play regularly – usually matches against other caddies for a few pfennigs. From the start he found golf more of a challenge than any other sport he had tried. Despite spending almost all his spare time on golf, he does not recall ever becoming bored with it.

Such was Bernhard's obsession with golf in those days that he would sometimes play two rounds of golf and caddy for another round, all in the course of one day. At times he even caddied for two people simultaneously – carrying one bag and pulling the other in a trolley! During the summer he sometimes camped in the wood by the club in order to save himself the cycle ride in the morning.

Over the next six years Bernhard spent as much time as possible at the golf club – practising relentlessly, learning by watching the better club members. But he had still not had a formal lesson, nor had he read any golf magazines or instruction books. As golf was such a minority sport in Germany he did not even have the opportunity of watching any of the stars of the game on television. Nonetheless by the age of 14 he was able to shoot scores in the low 70s at Augsburg.

Bernhard grew up in a family where belief in God and church-going were very much part of life. He noticed how his parents got strength from their faith. Bernhard feels that the roots of his own faith go back to this time. "I have always believed in God and always had a certain amount of faith." As a boy he went to church regularly and was an altar-boy for several years.

As he approached school-leaving age, Bernhard was sure that he wanted to earn his living in golf. But when he told the careers' adviser at the local job centre that he wanted to be a golf pro, he was asked, "What is a golf pro?" Undaunted, Bernhard remained resolute. When one of the members of the Augsburg club told him of a club in Munich – one and a half hours drive from Anhausen – which had a vacancy for an assistant professional, it was the opening that he was looking for.

He persuaded his parents to let him apply for the job and he was offered a contract by the club, just before his fifteenth birthday. At the club his duties involved working in the pro shop selling golf equipment, and giving lessons to the members. He also had to learn his trade, which involved day release study at the local college to take a course on business as well as English lessons. But the club also gave him time to practise and play the course. Under the critical eye of head professional, Heinz Fehring, he changed his grip and his stance to the ball and improved his technique.

The normal way to progress in golf is as an amateur member of a club. Then when one reaches a certain standard, one becomes a professional. Bernhard's experience was different. He was never an amateur. He went straight from being a caddy to being a professional. As a result of not playing amateur golf, he did not have the experience of playing in amateur competitive golf. As a result he had no idea how good he was in comparison with others of the same age. His thoughts on going to Munich were just to learn a profession that he could do for the rest of his life. During the three years he was there he started to play a few tournaments.

At the age of 16 he played in a competition involving professionals and amateurs from four German golf clubs. To everyone's surprise he won it, beating some of Germany's best professionals. The following year, 1975, he won the German National Open and decided that it was time to launch himself on the European Tour.

His success in the German National Championship gained him a sponsor who offered to pay him a regular wage in return for half his prize-money. He decided to give it two or three years to see if he could make it.

In February 1976 he set off for Portugal to play in his first European Tour event, the Portuguese Open. Over the next few months he was to discover that being number 1 in Germany would not impress the seasoned professionals on the European Tour and that the life of the touring professional is not as glamorous as it might appear from the outside. Travelling on a low budget, he could not afford to stay in a decent hotel. Looking back now he can see the funny side of it. He remarks that he would not send his dog to some of the hotels he stayed in during that period!

He missed the cut in the Portuguese Open and again in the Spanish Open. However, in his third tournament, the Madrid Open, he finished fifth. He ended the season 90th in the Order of Merit with a total prize money of

£2,130. It was hardly earth-shattering stuff yet at the age of 19 he was playing in the big league and gaining valuable experience.

The 1977 season was largely taken up with National Service and a back injury sustained on a military manoeuvre. As a result his appearances on the tour were limited. From then on, however, steady progress was made.

In 1978 he was 40th in Europe, in 1979 he was 56th but he also won the Cacharel Under-25s tournament. Then in 1980 came the real breakthrough.

Bernhard's spiritual state at this time is not easy to sum up. While his faith went with him into the world of tournament golf, somehow believing in God was never quite the top priority. He puts it like this: "Somewhere I reached a point where I was in nowhereland. I was believing and yet I was not 100 per cent sure. I still believed but I would not say that I had a personal relationship with God. I wasn't spending the time I should to read the Word and that kind of stuff. It was probably more a routine that I grew up with than anything else."

In 1980 Bernhard finished ninth in the European Order of Merit and he won his first European Tour event, the Dunlop Masters at St Pierre, Chepstow, in Wales. With scores of 70, 65, 67 and 68, he led from the second day and in the end won comfortably from Brian Barnes, who finished five strokes behind. The win was the culmination of a phenomenal three-week period in which he played 12 competitive rounds at Moortown, RAC Epsom and St Pierre at an average of 67.83.

The following year Bernhard Langer established himself as the number 1 player in Europe. He won the German Open and also finished second in the (British) Open Championship. But one curious incident in 1981 brought him more to the public's attention than his tournament successes.

During the Benson and Hedges International Tournament at Fulford he saw his approach to the 17th hole miss the green and hit a tree. The ball did not drop but remained sitting in a fork of the tree. Rather than declaring the ball unplayable and dropping another ball at the cost of a stroke, Benhard elected to climb the tree and chip the ball on to the green. The incident was shown on TV across the world with commentators wondering if he had used his "tree iron"!

So in 1981 at the age of 24 and in his sixth year on the tour, Bernhard had made it to number 1 in Europe. All the hopes that he had cherished during the difficult years of 1976 and 1977 when he was barely in the top 100 in Europe had now come to fruition. Originally Bernhard had set himself the goal of being the best player in Germany – already he had surpassed that.

In March 1983 while playing in a tournament in Florida, Bernhard went to dinner with an American player and some of his friends. Among the party was a girl called Vikki. Before the dinner had ended Bernhard had obtained Vikki's phone number and arranged another date. Vikki, who was working as a stewardess with Eastern Airlines at the time, managed to schedule her days off to suit Bernhard's tournaments. In addition, they were at times keeping the telephone company profitable by themselves!

As the relationship developed Vikki decided to travel on the tour with Bernhard for six weeks to sample the life of the tournament golfer. They were engaged in September and married on 21st January, 1984, in the church in Anhausen where Bernhard had been an altar-boy. It was a traditional German wedding, which meant a few shocks for Vikki. The first one was that the wedding cake was a chocolate cake – as opposed to one with white icing as Vikki might have expected.

The second shock was being kidnapped by Bernhard's brother. The tradition is that the bride is kidnapped from the wedding reception and the groom has to search until he finds her – normally drinking champagne with a group of friends. Tradition then demands that the groom pays the bill!

While winning any golf tournament is an achievement worthy of note, golfers tend to be judged by their performance in the four major championships – the US Master's, the US Open, the Open Championship (British Open), and the USPGA. In 1985 Bernhard broke into the exclusive class of major winners. He won the US Master's in 1985. While the other major tournaments have a different venue each year, the Master's is always held at the Augusta National Golf Club in Augusta, Georgia.

Curtis Strange seemed to have the 1985 Master's title already in his grasp when he led by four shots with just nine holes to play. Never was the old maxim, that the tournament doesn't really start until the last nine holes, more true.

With rounds of 72, 74, 68, Bernhard was joint third behind Ray Floyd and Curtis Strange and equal with Seve Ballesteros when the final round began. In the morning Bernhard and his wife Vikki went to a nearby church to pray about the day ahead. Inexplicably, they found it locked so they returned to the house where they were staying and prayed there. They hoped the day would get better!

When Strange stretched his lead to four strokes, Bernhard's chance seemed to have gone. Then Strange put his ball in water at the 13th and 15th holes. Meanwhile Langer made four birdies in the last seven holes to win by two shots from Strange, Ballesteros and Floyd, who finished equal second. He had become the third non-American – after Gary Player and Seve Ballesteros – to win the US Master's title.

Bernhard's win did cause a few problems to his coach, Willi Hofmann. Hofmann had watched the opening holes of the final round before setting off for the airport and his flight back to Germany. As he sat on the plane awaiting take-off he heard the pilot announce the result of the Master's. He persuaded the crew to allow him to leave the plane and he returned quickly to Augusta National to join in the celebrations.

After a celebration dinner at the Augusta National club, Bernhard and Vikki went to visit some friends. They went home and still unable to sleep spent part of the night and early morning walking together around Augusta.

The significance of the win – particularly in the eyes of the American golf establishment – was summed up by John Hopkins in the *Sunday Times*: "Two weeks ago he had been a rising professional on the US tour. Seventeen victories around the world hardly cut much ice . . . Augusta changed all that. Now the world is his oyster."

So far Bernhard has not added a second major victory, although, looking back, there have been a number of occasions when it could have happened. In 1981 he was second in the Open Championship at Sandwich, four shots behind Bill Rogers.

In 1984 at St Andrews he went even closer, finishing two shots behind Seve Ballesteros. On the final round his golf from tee to green, in the words of Mitchell Platts in *The Times*, "sparked like the sun on St Andrew's Bay". However his chance of winning evaporated on the greens where he failed to make five putts of 10 feet or under. The was third to Sandy Lyle at Sandwich in 1985 and to Greg Norman at Turnberry in 1986.

His best performance in the US Open was fourth in 1987 at San Francisco, when he finished six shots behind winner Scott Simpson.

Over the years Bernhard had made steady progress in his career. Initially he had set himself the target of being the best German, then he wanted to hold his own as a player on the European tour, then to become an exempt player (the top 60).

The next ambition was to be in the top 10 in Europe and then to win a tournament and to become the top player in Europe. The next goal was to succeed beyond Europe, to play on the US tour.

Playing in America proved to be a turning point in other aspects of his life, too. He developed friendships with players like Larry Nelson, Paul Azinger, Bobby Clampett, Larry Mize and with Larry Moody who runs the Bible Study on the US golf tour. He started to go regularly to the tour Bible Study. He enjoyed it. Gradually his priorities changed and God became Number One in his life. He watched Scott Simpson, who was to win the 1987 US Open, work his way through tough issues to commitment to Christ and soon this was his experience, too. Having appreciated the support of the Bible Study in America, Bernhard longed to see one in Europe too. The need was clear. As he puts it himself: "If you play in a tournament which finishes on a Sunday every week, when are you ever going to get to church and how are you going to grow spiritually?"

One of the great success stories of the 'eighties has been Europe's breaking of the American stranglehold on the Ryder Cup. First introduced in 1927, the Ryder Cup was contested between the professional golfers of Great Britain and the USA every second year, with the venue alternating between the two countries. From 1979 onwards America has faced the golfers of Europe (rather than just Britain). The competition is held over three days with foursomes, fourballs and singles, making a total of 28 individual matches to decide the destiny of the trophy.

When Bernhard first earned the right to a place in the European team in 1981, America had last been beaten in 1957 (and before that in 1933) and had won 19 of the 23 contests. The USA had a comfortable win in 1981 at Walton Heath 18½ to 9½.

In 1983 in Florida Europe made a monumental effort to regain the cup. Bernhard partnered Nick Faldo in the foursome and fourballs, winning three and losing one. Bernhard also won his singles, beating Jay Haas. The score was 13–13 with two matches to finish, but the USA just pulled through 14½ to 13½.

In 1985 at the Belfry near Birmingham the European team entered the competition with more confidence than ever. Playing with four different partners in the four foursomes and fourballs, Bernhard held his own – a win, a defeat and two halves. He beat Hal Sutton in the singles. Amidst scenes of great excitement, Europe won the match and the cup 16½ to 11½. This marked the start of a new era in international golf.

The Ryder Cup was retained in 1987 at Muirfield Village, Columbus, Ohio, when Europe won 15–13. Langer won three out of four foursomes/fourballs and then halved with Larry Nelson in the singles. The match ended with both players hitting iron shots on to the green close to the flag. Rather than insisting on seeing the putts holed in the hope that the opponent would miss, the players mutually decided, in the spirit of sportsmanship expected of the Ryder Cup, to concede the opponent's putt and settle for a halved match.

The 1989 Ryder Cup at the Belfry finished 14–14 so

Europe retained their grip on the cup for the third time in a row. One memorable aspect of the 1989 Ryder Cup was the service held on the 18th Green on the Sunday morning before play started.

Before describing that in detail, however, it is necessary to retrace our steps to an incident at the beginning of the 1989 golf season. One week in May Bernhard was at a prayer meeting in Germany. Bernhard's prayer request was that a Bible Study would be started in the European golf tour. Later that week he travelled to Wales to play in the Epsom tournament. On the Wednesday, just before he went out to play in the Pro-am, his caddy, Peter Coleman, told him that there were three people outside who wanted to see him about a Bible Study. He could hardly believe it.

Bruce Gillingham, diocesan missioner in the Birmingham diocese, accompanied by two colleagues from Christians in Sport (alias the authors if this book), told him that they were keen to start a regular Bible Study on the tour. Bernhard suggested that they hold the first one at the PGA Championship at Wentworth later that month.

The Bible Study at Wentworth had a false start. It was scheduled for the Wedneday but play was rained off and the Bible Study was postponed to the following day. Bernhard arranged a room in the PGA European Tour headquarters at Wentworth and put up a notice in the locker room. After that it was just a case of waiting. Another player and his wife attended. The encouraging thing was that the Bible Study had got under way.

Under a headline "No driving for Jesus", a cynical piece in the *Independent* stated that "the European tour was being invited to get religion" and stated, inaccurately, that not one player had responded to the invitation. In fact it was the start of a series. Players' Bible

Studies were held at six tournaments in 1989, including a special reception for European and American golfers at the Open Championship at Troon.

In 1990 more than 30 attended a similar gathering at St Andrews, the home of golf, to hear an address by Bruce Gillingham and music by Martyn Joseph. In addition to the tournaments which Bruce Gillingham is able to get to, Bernhard Langer and Gavin Levinson now lead Bible Studies at every tournament they play, usually with between six and twelve attending.

The theme of the 1990 Bible Studies was "Following Jesus, a study of people close to Jesus". The study was based on Mark's Gospel, known to the players as the "card of the course". In 1991 they studied Philippians.

Vikki Langer, who has been such a source of strength to Bernhard, has started a Bible Study for the wives on tour. They all appreciate the chance to talk over their own concerns. Together they make plans for charity events which sponsor children with special needs.

The players' Bible Study is now an accepted part of the tour. This was confirmed by a remark by Ken Schofield, Director of the PGA Tour, in connection with the phasing out of appearance money at tournaments. He said, "If Bernhard doesn't agree, I'll charge him a fee for his church services on the 18th green."

At the 1989 Ryder Cup a Bible Study was planned for the Friday evening for players from both teams. On the Thursday evening Bernhard and Vikki met Bruce Gillingham to finalise the arrangements for the study. It was there that the idea of a service arose. Bruce mentioned that he was preaching at a church very close to the Belfry on the Sunday morning and suggested that some of the players' wives might like to come. Bernhard replied, "Bruce, I think we can do better than that. Let's have a service here at the Belfry." Bernhard approached the PGA officials with the idea. At first they were surprised at the request but in the end they agreed to consider it as a committee.

On the Saturday morning permission was given and Bruce Gillingham hastily started to make the necessary arrangements – PA system, music, publicity, security passes for those taking part, etc.

The service took place by the 18th green on the Sunday morning from 9.15am to 10.00am. Chris de Burgh, who was staying at the Belfry, accepted Bernhard's invitation to sing two songs, Paul Azinger and Bernhard read the lessons and Bruce Gillingham spoke on "Peace under pressure". Benhard had chosen to read from Philippians chapter four, which included a verse which had meant a great deal to him during the problems that he had faced with his golf: "I can do everything through Him who gives me the strength." In addition to the players and officials who attended, the service was enjoyed by the considerable gallery in the stands and heard by the crowd as it was broadcast over the PA system.

Bernhard was delighted with the service: "I thought it was great that in the midst of the fierce competition, believers from both teams could sit together, believing in the same God."

This sentiment was captured by some of the photographers and a photo appeared in the next day's *Daily Mail* of Bernhard sharing a Bible with Paul Azinger. The caption on the picture was "Love thy neighbour". In 1991 during the PGA championship another Sunday service was held on the 18th green, the first one at a European Tour tournament.

Bernhard's success on the golf course has brought him a great deal of money. In addition to his prize money there are lucrative contracts with BOSS clothing, Wilson golf clubs, Adidas shoes, etc. The lifestyle of a top golfer is, however, not always as exciting as people may think.

Bernhard finds the travelling and being away from home "the hardest part of the job. Living in hotel rooms – even the best hotels with all the luxury that they can provide – is no comparison with home."

Away from the golf course, skiing is one of the great loves of Bernhard's life. He is a very accomplished skier. Because of the risk of injury, however, he always has to plan his skiing trips to give time to recover before the next important golf tournament. Christmas is an important time of family relaxation. Bernhard tries to take a month off, some of which is spent skiing and playing tennis, another of his great loves.

Bernhard plays about 35 tournaments a year – in all parts of the world. Add to that the time taken by sponsors and business meetings and he is left with no more than ten or twelve weeks at home in the year. In 1984 Bernhard married Vikki and they now have two children, Jackie (born in 1986) and Stefan (born in 1990). As far as possible the Langers travel as a family. As Bernhard says when he arrives to play a golf tournament somewhere, it is not so much a courtesy car as a courtesy truck that needs to meet him at the airport.

People sometimes wonder how golfers or tennis players motivate themelves to travel endlessly to play against the same people as last week and the week before. This is not a difficulty for Bernhard: "I have never had a problem with motivation. I have somewhere within me something that makes me want always to try my best. The only time I find it hard is when I have played too much – say eight to ten weeks running – then it is easy to say to yourself 'what am I doing here, I wish I could just go home.' With experience, however, you learn how to pace yourself and take enough breaks in the schedule."

Vikki was an air hostess before she married Bernhard, so she was used to a life of constant travel. She has accepted their lifestyle, apparently without problems. She jokes "I am not sure that I would like him to have a nine-to-five job. That way I would have to cook dinner every night!"

One of the things people associate with Bernhard Langer is putting and the yips. The yips is a condition that afflicts golfers at all levels on the putting green. It is an inability to control the putter or the ball on short putts which the player would normally expect to hole without any problem. It is a churning of the stomach, a condition of extreme nervousness which can almost prevent a player from moving the putter or force him to jerk the club. Bernhard developed the problem first in about 1977. At times it has got so bad that he has taken four putts from 6 feet. Bernhard sees the origins of the problem in the transition from playing in Germany to other countries: "All my life until then I had putted on slow greens in Germany. Then suddenly I was faced with the really fast greens of Portugal and Spain. I just did not know what to do. I could not handle it. I made lots of three-putts, then I became discouraged, scared and uptight. It got worse and worse."

In his book *When the Iron is Hot*, Bernhard describes it clearly: "I began to lose control of my putter as soon as I got close to the hole . . . People were coming out to watch me play but it was in the manner of those people who go to car races hoping to see a crash . . . I rarely let them down. To the spectators it must have been like watching a man suffer a very public nervous breakdown as I stood over my ball, muscles tensing, colour draining from my face."

During this period he received suggestions from every quarter – hypnosis, a new putter, a new grip, or hold the putter looser, and so on. Bernhard's own solution was characteristic – he worked harder than ever. He spent hour after hour on the practice putting green. He conquered the problem to such an extent that he had the successes described above in 1980 and 1981.

In 1982 putting became a problem again. In his book he wrote about being "plunged into the depths of near despair when my putting suddenly disintegrated again."

Bernhard's reaction was again hard work, this time with a new grip with the left hand below the right. By the end of the season he felt that he was putting better than ever. The official tour statistics for 1984 recorded that with 28.84 putts per round, he was the best putter in Europe.

Putting problems resurfaced again in 1988. At that time he might travel to a tournament with as many as a dozen putters. Ultimately he adopted another new technique which involves gripping the left arm with the right hand, trapping the shaft of the putter against the left forearm. He uses the conventional grip on long putts but reverts to the new approach on shorter putts.

Nontheless Bernhard Langer's putting remains part of golf's mythology. There was the journalist who wrote, "The greens were so good that even Bernhard Langer did not three-putt on them." At times he is irritated by this. "The Press like to give you a label and you can't get rid of it. I was winning tournaments and playing very well, yet still the press kept saying 'that is the distance he doesn't like'. It annoys me at times." But many golf writers have written about his courage and perseverance in over-coming, three times in his career putting problems that would have sunk a lesser man.

The irony is that in 1990, not for the first time, he came top of the European putting statistics. That is, he took less putts per round than any other player.

Bernhard feels that three things brought him through

those dark days: personal support from family and friends; iron discipline and the courage to practise; and a deep trust in the acceptance of Christ. Now he can see the value of the experience and readily admits that he learnt a lot and saw his faith grow more during the hard times than in the successes.

Bernhard Langer has been one of the outstanding golfers in the world in the 'eighties. He put German golf on the map, being the first German to reach world class. For a period in 1986 and 1987 he was arguably the best golfer in the world. He has won over 30 tournaments around the world, including the prestigious US Master's.

His record would be remarkable enough for anyone. Given his background, the country of his birth and the putting problems that have beset him, it is a phenomenal achievement that he has reached and stayed at the top. Looking back Bernhard feels that the only goal that he ever set himself which has not been fulfilled is to win all the majors.

He has put his success at the service of Christ and there seems no reason why he will not remain a force in world golf for many years to come and go on to win more major tournaments.

CAREER SUMMARY

Tournament wins

1979	Cacharel Under-25s Championship
1980	Dunlop Masters
	Columbian Open
1981	German Open
	Bob Hope British Classic
1982	Lufthansa German Open
1983	Johnnie Walker Tournament
	Casio World Open (Japan)
	Italian Open
	Glasgow Golf Classic
	St Mellion Timeshare TPC
1984	Peugeot French Open
	KLM Dutch Open
	Carrolls Irish Open
	Benson and Hedges Spanish Open
1985	Lufthansa German Open
	Panasonic European Open
	US Master's
	Australian Master's
	Sea Pines Heritage Classic
1986	German Open
	Lancome Trophy (Tied)
1987	Whyte and Mackay PGA Championship
	Carrolls Irish Open
1988	Epson Grand Prix
1989	German Master's
	Peugeot Spanish Open
1990	Madrid Open
	Austrian Open
1991	Hong Kong Open
	Benson and Hedges International

Teams

Ryder Cup 1981, 83, 85, 87, 89
Hennessey 1976, 78, 80, 82
World Cup 1976, 77, 78, 79, 80
Nissan Cup 1985, 86
Kirin Cup 1987
Asahi Cup 1989
World Cup 1990 (Germany Winners)

Ranking

Top European Order of Merit 1981, 1984
Best World Ranking 2 (1986–87)

LISA OPIE

In the spring of 1989, Lisa Opie shocked the squash world by announcing that she was taking a complete break from the game for three months. An unexpected defeat by Sarah Fitzgerald in the second round of the British Open – in a match in which she had been leading by two games to nil, against an opponent whom she should have beaten relatively easily – was the last straw that confirmed Lisa's growing conviction that years of constant travel and competition had taken their toll, leaving her stale and jaded. She needed out.

After ten years on the circuit during which she had never managed more than three or four weeks off at one time, she felt bored with the continuous round of tournaments and in need of a complete break in order to regain her appetite for squash.

Moreover Lisa had become a Christian some months earlier and was convinced that God "wanted me to take time off to get to know Him better. Since becoming a Christian everything had been a rush. I didn't give the Lord enough time. I became run-down. I was over-doing things."

A holiday in Turkey was followed by a month in Guernsey, helping out in her parents' pottery business and generally doing very little except enjoy the idyllic scenery of the countryside and secluded coves of the coast around Moulin Huet valley near her parents' home. This was followed by two months' training in Nottingham before launching herself on the tournament circuit.

In the middle of her lay-off, Richard Eaton wrote of Lisa being in crisis and asked "Will she ever be quite the same player again?" But the break seemed to do the trick as Lisa quickly regained her form and appetite and her World Ranking of Number 2.

Lisa was born in Guernsey in August 1963. Both her parents were Channel Islanders, Rex being from Guernsey and his wife, Robina, from Jersey. The family's only claim to sporting prowess was that Robina had represented the Channel Islands at table tennis in the 1958 Commonwealth Games in Cardiff.

Rex Opie introduced his daughter to squash when she was aged 11. They played at the Elizabeth College, which at that time had the only squash court on the island. When the King's Club opened at St Peter Port, Lisa and her father continued their squash matches there. Her potential for the game was such that at the age of 12 she was invited to practise with the England junior squad, who were in a training camp in Guernsey.

From then on she was hooked on squash. She recalls that there was pressure at school to play team sports, but somehow she never quite managed to turn up for hockey or netball practice – she was always playing squash.

From the age of 13 Lisa settled into a pattern of school on Monday to Thursday with Friday being spent travelling to the mainland to play squash. The price of her success at squash was not quite fitting in at school. Always being away at weekends meant missing out on her friends' social life. She often felt awkward at school on a Monday. The school she attended was a convent school but she had no real interest in the religious aspects of school life.

A notable achievement in this period was her first victory over her father. Lisa recalls: "He took it like a man – he sulked." Further progress was indicated when she reached the semi-final of the British Girls' Championship.

A less enjoyable occasion was when she knocked herself out when she was 13. It was ironically the first time her grandma had come to watch her play. She ran into a wall, got concussion and was taken off to hospital.

After completing her 'O' levels, Lisa was faced with a dilemma. Should she stay on to take 'A' levels or should she stop letting school get in the way of squash? If she had stayed on at school, art college would have been the probable course of the next few years. It was a hard decision as the Opies were a close-knit family and Lisa was particularly close to sister Karla, just 16 months younger. Despite the family ties, however, she chose squash and in 1980, aged 17, she turned professional and moved to Nottingham where she joined up with John and Richard Le Lievre, other Guernsey exiles.

The first year in Nottingham was tough but then she went to live with John and Mary Vaulkhard and began to settle down and feel at home. She stayed with them for three years.

For an island of some 50,000 to produce two of the world's top women squash players hardly seems credible, but that is what Guernsey has done. One of Lisa's first regular opponents when she started to play squash was Martine Le Moignan, who is just one year older than Lisa. It is a curiosity that Martine and Lisa, who were born in the same hospital, attended the same infants and junior schools, played at the same squash clubs – first in Guernsey and then in Nottingham – should, years later, still play matches against each other in far-flung corners of the globe as the world's number two and four players.

Guernsey's contribution to Women's Squash was

recognised in 1989 when two special challenge matches took place between Guernsey and the rest of the World. The first was drawn but the World won the second. A further indication of Guernsey being placed firmly on the map was the addition in 1990 of the Guernsey Ladies' Open to the tournament schedule. It was one of those rare tournaments when the final was eclipsed by the semi-final. When Martine and Lisa met in the semis, this was the match that everyone on the island wanted to see. Lisa won 9-4, 9-5, 9-3 to be crowned unofficial champion of Guernsey. That Lisa lost the final somehow did not seem to matter so much.

Lisa's decision to move from Guernsey to Nottingham was rewarded the following year, 1981, when she won the World Junior title in Ottawa, defeating Martine Le Moignan in the final. The same year she also reached the semi-final of the World Open. That year she was ranked number 1 in England.

Apart from a few brief periods when Martine Le Moignan has displaced her – as did Lucy Soutter for a time in 1985 – Lisa has remained from then to the present the officially ranked Number 1 player in Britain. By 1981 she had achieved a world ranking of three and has remained ranked two or three in the world more or less ever since.

Leaving behind all her friends, family and familiar things threw Lisa on to her own resources. She has become self-sufficient, happy with her own company. She lives on her own – although her flat has over the years become a haven for overseas squash players who are spending a period in Nottingham. Friends who telephone Lisa have learnt not to be surprised to be greeted by an antipodean voice on the other end of the line. She still trains on her own and does not currently employ a coach. She worked with Jonah Barrington,

Britain's best ever male squash player, from 1983–85 and acknowledges the value of this period. In the longer term, however, she feels that she "gets confused if I have people telling me what to do all the time. I don't know whether to follow my instincts or try to do what they say – in the end I don't know what to think. Now I just listen to myself."

An example of this came on a trip to Australia in 1986. The trip was intended as a playing/training trip, designed to sharpen her game for the coming season. But it was not that simple: "Suddenly I found myself going through a very bad patch on and off court. I was playing badly and that was getting me down. I realised that, if I did not do something about it, the trip was going to turn into a very expensive waste of time. I had no one to lean on – no coach, no family or whatever – so I knew I had to work it out by myself. I did and it was probably the best thing that could have happened to me."

When she is at home Lisa trains six days a week. Most days she will do a "physical" session – a long run, a series of sprints, weights, etc. She will also play a match – normally against a county standard man. For variation she sometimes practises her shots alone in the squash court. When she launched herself on the squash circuit Lisa was much heavier than she is now. A rigorous training schedule sustained over the years has now made her one of the fittest and fastest players in the game.

In the final of the British Open in 1984, an incident took place which has haunted Lisa ever since. Top seed for the tournament, she progressed to the final quite comfortably – inevitably defeating Le Moignan on the way. Lisa lost the final to Susan Devoy of New Zealand 9–5, 0–9, 7–9, 1–9. The crucial point of the match came in the third game. At one game all and 8–7 to Devoy, the referee awarded a stroke to Susan Devoy, so giving her the third game. As she left the court between the third and fourth games, Lisa flung a V-sign in the direction of the referee, Bob Johnson. She was instantly warned that if the gesture was repeated the match would be awarded to her opponent.

At the end of the match – which was screened live on BBC television – Lisa threw her racket over the back wall of the all-transparent perspex court and into the crowd where the referee was sitting. Writing in *Squash Player International*, Larry Halpin, while not in any way condoning Lisa's behaviour, commented: "There is no doubt that she was under severe pressure throughout the tournament and the disappointment of finishing runner-up for the third year in a row must have been a bitter pill indeed to swallow."

The following weekend she appeared on the BBC TV programme, Grandstand, to offer a public apology. Nonetheless, she was fined £1,000 and banned from the following year's British Open. Jean Reynolds, chairman of the Women's Squash Rackets Association, commented that the fine was intended to deprive Lisa of her prize money from the tournament (£1,375), taking account of expenses.

An appeal was heard by Sue Mappin (British Women's Tennis manager), Janet Richardson (a veteran player) and Maeve Feeney (a current player). The panel reduced the fine to £100 but upheld the ban. Part of the reason for the reduction in the fine was that the original disciplinary committee had, incredibly, not been aware that the WSRA code of conduct only permitted a maximum fine of £100.

Looking back Lisa deeply regrets the incident, pointing out that she was 20 when it happened, that she apologised publicly at the time and has not sought to defend her actions. "Obviously I shouldn't have thrown that racket. Things just happened on the spur of the moment. It didn't do me much good over the next few years." She is irritated that this is the incident with which she is associated rather than her tournament wins. BBC TV, for example, in their report of the 1990 British Open, showed the racket-throwing incident – in a way which could have implied that it had taken place in 1990 rather than 1984.

The official programme of the 1990 British Open gave equal prominence to the incident, advising spectators who watched Lisa to "bring a tin hat and be prepared to duck". Profile articles on her have appeared in *The Times* under the headlines of "The tempest from the Channel" and "From spoiled brat to darling girl". While Lisa has certainly had her problems on the court, they were almost exclusively several years ago and, most people would say, springing from frustration at her failure to realise her full potential rather than from any malice towards the umpire, her opponents or anyone else.

On Lisa's mantelpiece in Nottingham, the incident is commemorated by a small statue of Lisa with racket in one hand making a V-sign with the other! It's a present from her sister who works in the family pottery in Guernsey.

The 1984 British Open heralded the start of a difficult period in Lisa's career. There was constant pressure from the press, who seemed always to be on the look-out for any sign of tantrum on the court. Then she contracted hepatitis. She lost her Number 1 UK ranking.

The 1986 National Championship was when it all came good. As Larry Halpin wrote in *Squash World*: "It was a performance that firmly established her as Britain's best player." In the semi-final she beat the defending champion Lucy Soutter. In the final Martine Le Moignan was despatched 9–7, 9–1, 9–0. Lisa enjoyed herself at the press conference following the win. "There isn't one of you who hasn't written me off at some stage", she told the gathering journalists. She added, "It's good to be back", with a mocking smile – making the press eat their words as she reminded them that it was they who had decided that she had gone away in the first place!

She has won the National Championships four times – 1981, 1983, 1986 and 1987. The 1987 final in which she beat Lucy Soutter 6–9, 5–9, 9–2, 9–0, 9–4 included a six-minute break when Lisa accidentally struck Soutter across the face with her racket and the latter had to receive treatment for a nosebleed. This prompted one headline: "Opie by a nose".

The British Open, squash's equivalent of Wimbledon, was for many years a tournament in which Lisa never seemed able to do herself justice. She could win abroad yet somehow the pressure of the home crowd, etc., also seemed to get to her in her own open. She first played in the British Open in 1980 when she lost in the second round to Lesley Chapman 1–3.

In the 1981 British Open Lisa reached the semi-final, losing to Margaret Zachariah, an immensely experienced player from Australia, 9–6, 10–8 and 9–6. The match was closer than the score suggests as Lisa led 6–5 in the first and third games as well as reaching 8–8 in the second. She also had the misfortune to be struck in the face by her opponent's racket. However, her performance was sufficient to prompt the Canadian national coach, Tony Swift, to remark: "Lisa is the most intelligent player I have seen in this tournament. She moves the ball beautifully, has her opponent going to all corners and varies the pace nicely."

She reached the final three years in a row, in 1982, 1983 and 1984, without ever being able quite to pull it off.

'In 1982 she reached the final by defeating Barbara Oldfield – whose name crops up later in the chapter – in the semi-final. Her success was partly attributed to a pink piglet mascot, which had watched from the court side! On a tour to Canada, Lisa had been the youngest – and most overweight – member of the party. As a result the others called her "piglet", and one of them bought her the pig!

She lost the final to Vicki Cardwell (Australia) 4–9, 9–3, 9–4, 9–4. Cardwell, who had also won the title in 1980 and 1981, was fulsome in her praise of Lisa. She said at the end of the final, "I praised Lisa in 1980 and she got better, I praised her in 1981 and she got better again. Now I think it is time I stopped praising her!"

Lisa entered the 1983 British Open at the Assembly Rooms in Derby full of confidence. She had already won the East of England and South of England Open titles, defeating the World Champion, Rhonda Thorne of Australia, in both. A semi-final win over Angela Smith put her in the final against Vicki Cardwell, a repeat of the previous year. Lisa won the first game and led 6–4 in the second before going down 10–9, 6–9, 4–9, 5–9. Lisa had to be satisfied with Cardwell's praise and prediction, "Lisa will be the next World Number 1 for sure. There was never any point that I was absolutely sure of winning." Lisa's own view of the match was she had "needed somebody to tell me that I could win".

In the 1984 British Open, Lisa beat Martine in the semi-final before losing to Susan Devoy in the final with the racket throw incident.

Lisa reached the semi-final of the 1985 British Open – the ban had been lifted due to her good disciplinary record in the previous year. She lost 9–10, 7–9, 7–9 to Martine Le Moignan, who had taken over from her as UK Number 1 and World Number 2. The match was frustrating for Lisa as she had led 6–1 and 8–5 in the first game and 7–3 in the second, only to snatch defeat from the jaws of victory. But in view of the previous year it was just a relief to get through the tournament without incident.

In 1986 she again reached the final, beating Alison Cummings in the quarter-final and Lucy Soutter in the semi-final, after being 2–0 down, only to be swept aside in the final 4–9, 2–9, 3–9 by Susan Devoy in 36 minutes. *Squash Player International!* summed up her performance in the 1986 British Open: "Despite a fourth unsuccessful final, Lisa scored a personal victory in her entire approach to the pressures of the event and her remarkable win over Lucy Soutter (who had taken over Lisa's English Number 1 ranking a few months prior to the tournament). Remarkable not because she won, for the outcome of any match between any of the British top five could not be predicted for certain, but because Lisa was 0–2 down and then played the match of her life. After that she could be forgiven for not finding the where-withall to overcome Devoy."

For the next four years she failed to justify her seeding in the Open. In 1987 she lost 3–1 to Liz Irving in the quarter-final. The following year she lost in the same round to Martine Le Moignan 3–1. In 1989, she lost to Sarah FitzGerald 9–4, 9–6, 6–9, 4–9, 9–10 – even having two match balls in the final game. In 1990 she lost in the quarter-final to Michelle Martin 5–9, 9–6, 4–9, 9–2, 2–9.

Lisa admitted as much after the 1990 defeat when she said "I am totally fed up. I've played well all season but yet again I've missed out in the most important tournament. Perhaps I put too much pressure on myself instead of relaxing as I do before other events."

In 1991 it all came right, at the eleventh attempt. She cruised into the semi-final where she met Martine Le Moignan. Lisa already had two good wins over Martine in 1991 in the Welsh Open and the National League.

However she had lost in their last meeting, in the Guernsey Open, when, admittedly, both players were recovering from flu. On this occasion the outcome was never in doubt with Lisa winning 4–9, 9–4, 9–3, 9–3.

In the final she met Sue Wright, a 20-year-old from Kent, who had defeated the numbers 1 and 3 seeds to reach the final. After a nervous start Lisa won 6–9, 9–3, 9–3, 9–4 in 44 minutes. At last she was British Open champion and, to put the icing on the cake, it was a royal occasion with the Duke of Edinburgh making the presentation. As the Men's World Number One, Jahangir Khan, said at the presentation ceremony "About time too!"

In August 1988 she was playing in New Zealand and went out to stay with an old squash-player friend, Barbara Oldfield, for four days in Sydney. The visit was to change her life. Unknown to Lisa at the time, Barbara had been praying for her for some time – in fact she had previously taken her to church but it had no effect on her.

"On the Sunday, Barbara asked me to come to church with her and I went. All the way through I was pouring with sweat and at the end went out to the front. I was in tears and I gave my life to the Lord there and then. The former Wimbledon champion, Margaret Court, who was a church member there, took me into a little room and explained that Jesus had died to take away my sins and that all I had to do was to accept His offer of forgiveness and have faith in Him. I had a flight to catch about three hours later. So I went back for lunch and they both gave me some books and tapes and off I went to the next tournament. It was all a bit rushed really."

"But by the time I came back to Nottingham, Margaret Court had telephoned the tennis commentator, Gerald Williams, and he had set up a number of contacts in Nottingham for me. One of these was J John, an anglican evangelist. John and Killy have developed into very good friends and in fact I am godmother to their son Simeon. John recalls that Gerald Williams had warned him to be very wary of me as I was the John McEnroe of squash! The first thing John did was to give me ten Bible lessons. My first reaction was 'Oh no, this is like going back to school again' but it was really helpful. Looking back I am so grateful to have had someone like that looking after me from the start."

Other squash players started noticing that something was different about Lisa. One of the players said to Barbara, "Just wait till Lisa gets back to England, I bet she won't last two weeks before she has forgotten all about it." But when Barbara next saw her, she noticed that the Lisa she had played against "who was always ready to explode on court and whose language was appalling had become a lot more settled through experiencing the peace of God in her life".

If you are an aggressive "temperamental" player, how does it affect you when you become a Christian? Lisa explains, "Compared to before, I am like an angel on the court. However, I am still aggressive. I still question calls but now I am more able to control myself. What is difficult is that when I became a Christian, some people disapproved if I shouted on court or showed any aggression."

When she is in Nottingham Lisa attends church regularly as well as the Nottingham Christians in Sport group. The problem is that she is in Nottingham for only about half the year. When travelling, she makes a point of reading the Bible with her Bible Study notes. In addition to strengthening her faith this can be a witness to others. On one occasion in Singapore, she recalls leaving two fellow players in her hotel room looking up passages in the Bible while she went off to play a match.

On the same trip to Singapore, David Shearman from The Christian Centre had alerted two friends of his to her arrival. They were John and Mary Elliott, who lived in Singapore. As Lisa recalls, she had hardly had time to settle into her hotel room when the phone rang.

"Mary took me to church on the Sunday which was great as I don't often get the chance to go to church when I'm on tour. After church we had lunch and then she dropped me back at the squash centre. A press reporter saw me arrive and asked where I had been. I said, 'Church'. He looked surprised but asked me some more questions and eventually wrote an article 'Faith makes the difference'. To complete the week I won the Singapore Open!"

The World Open takes place on alternate years with the World team championship following it. In 1983 in Australia Lisa lost in the quarter-final of the individual to Rhonda Thorne 9–7, 9–6, 9–10, 3–9, 9–10. It was desperately frustrating to lose after being two games up and standing 9–9 in the third – and in the end only to lose 10–9 in the fifth – to an opponent whom she had beaten twice earlier in the year.

In the 1983 team championship, England reached the final but lost 2–1 to Australia, with Opie again losing to Thorne after being 2–1 up and standing 8–8 in the fourth. On the way to the final England had beaten New Zealand 3–0, with Lisa defeating Susan Devoy (9–3, 6–9, 9–1, 9–5).

In 1985 Lisa reached the final of the Seven-Up World Open in Dublin, beating Le Moignan in the semi-final before losing to Susan Devoy 4–9, 5–9, 8–10. England won the team event but Lisa, World Open runner-up just a few days before, was dropped from the England team. Manager Alex Cowie and coach, Malcolm Willstrop, were concerned about Lisa's form in the early rounds and concluded that the team's best chance of success in the competition lay with a team of Martine Le Moignan, Lucy Soutter and Alison Cumings.

Lisa got great support from the players in the Australian and New Zealand teams – she was offered a New Zealand tracksuit to replace her England one. To her credit Lisa sat with the England party and cheered her team to victory. At the prize-giving ceremony when the players were introduced, Lisa was given a foot-stamping reception while the England management were greeted only with polite applause from a section of the crowd.

In 1987 the Honda World Championships were held in Auckland. Seeded two in the individual event, Lisa defeated Vicki Cardwell in the semi-final but lost the final to Susan Devoy – 3–9, 8–10, 2–9. England won the team event with Lisa – omitted last time but now very much the heroine. Lisa won all her matches, including the defeat of Susan Devoy 9–6, 9–7, 1–9, 9–0 as England beat New Zealand in the semi-final. In the final England beat Australia 2–1 with Lisa repeating her individual win over Vicki Cardwell.

Under a headline of "Opie is the heroine", *Squash World* described Lisa's play as "squash of a standard rarely seen – long range drop shots, clever switches of play, beautifully judged lobs into the back corners . . ." Cardwell's comment after the two defeats was: "If Lisa continues to develop, she will not only be the most talented player in the world but also the best player in the world."

In the 1989 World Open in Germany, Lisa surprisingly lost 6–9, 5–9, 9–7, 9–0, 6–9 to Sarah FitzGerald in the third round. She regained her form in the team event, which England retained. As in Auckland two years before, Lisa had a 100 per cent record in the team event.

The next world championships were held in Australia

in October 1990 – just 18 months after the previous ones in order to switch them from spring to autumn. The tournament somehow encapsulated in three weeks the whole of Lisa's squash career.

Her preparation for the tournament could not have been better. She trained hard in Nottingham, then stopped off in the Far East just long enough to win the Open Championships of Malaysia and Singapore. She spent two weeks in Perth, staying with Barbara Oldfield, training and preparing before setting off for Sydney.

A strike at Perth airport threatened to disrupt her plans. The 7.00am flight on which she was booked was cancelled. The next flight was delayed. Despite Lisa's pleas about the World Championships, she was told that she had no chance of getting on a flight that day as she was fiftieth on the waiting list. But Barbara Oldfield told her, "Don't worry, I'm praying!" When Lisa returned in the afternoon she was told that the pilot had agreed to take her in the jump-seat in the cockpit, ahead of the people on the waiting list. A fellow squash player who had to wait until the next day remarked, "Typical Opie. She can talk her way out of anything!"

Seeded two in the tournament, she started well beating Hilary King 9–3, 9–2, 9–0 followed by Sabine Schone of Germany 9–1, 9–0, 9–2 in eight minutes. In the fourth round she met Sarah FitzGerald, who had previously proved to be something of a bogey player for Lisa. After a tense start she triumphed 8–10, 10–8, 8–10, 9–5, 9–3, in 86 minutes.

In the quarter-final she met Robin Lambourne of Australia. Lisa lost 9–10, 9–10, 9–4, 9–7, 7–9 in 85 minutes. She led 8–7 in both the opening games but lost them, fought back to 2–2 with some inspired squash, led 7–5 in the final game before disaster struck. Lambourne levelled to 7–7 and then the Australian referee, Chris

Sinclair, awarded two penalty points to Lambourne.

The standard of the refereeing was criticised from all sides throughout the tournament. This was the lowest point. Lisa found that Australian players apologised to her for the biased decisions in favour of the home player. Martine Le Moignan, due to meet the winner in the semi-final, watched the match: "I feel sorry for Lisa, that last decision was dreadful."

In the team competition England moved easily into the semi-final where they met New Zealand. Lisa was to face Susan Devoy, who had just won her third world championship. Playing with what Colin McQuillan called "brilliant athleticism and perception" she defeated Devoy 9–7, 9–2, 9–4 in just 34 minutes.

In the final England beat Australia 2–1 with Lisa defeating the world number 3 player, Danielle Drady, 9–4, 6–9, 9–6, 9–5. England had won the world team championships for the fourth successive time with Lisa maintaining her 100 per cent record in the last three team championships.

Lisa's impish sense of humour had clearly returned by this stage as she referred to Martine throughout the press conference as the queen!

Alex Cowie, the England team manager, was fulsome in her praise of Lisa. "The game against Danielle Drady was a real pressure match but Lisa handled the pressure. Before the team competition she said that she would not lose a match and she did it. She played brilliantly with skill, discipline and concentration and did not allow anything to distract her."

Lisa had yet again proved to be an enigma. She had failed to do herself justice in the individual championship, losing to the fifth seed. Moreover, she had lost from a winning position. Then in the semi-final and final of the team competition, she had beaten the world's number 1 and number 3 players. With the exception of the match she lost, she had probably played the best squash of her life during those three weeks. Yet she had once again come away empty-handed from the world championships.

Life on the professional squash circuit is not without its moments of amusement. In one tournament Lisa had played all her matches at 6.00pm. On the date of the final at just after 5.00pm, Lisa was pottering around in her hotel room before setting off for the Squash Centre. The telephone rang. The conversation went something like this.

"Where are you?"

"I'm in the hotel, just about to leave."

"Well, there are 2,000 people waiting to watch you and the match was due to start five minutes ago."

"Oh, help."

On another occasion Lisa was "knocked out" of a tournament in Paris. Stretching for a drop shot from Susan Devoy, Lisa tripped over her opponent's foot and crashed head first into the side wall. After a short break for treatment, Lisa returned to court with a lump on her head like you only see in cartoons. After playing for a few minutes it was obvious that Lisa was in no state to continue and she reluctantly withdrew from the tournament.

Once her bra-strap broke during a match. She discreetly whispered to her opponent the reason why she had to leave court for a moment. However, her opponent instantly informed the crowd of Lisa's problem, so adding to her embarrassment.

In 1990 she also enlisted the help of a sports psychologist, Graham Jones from Loughborough University. The areas on which she is working are relaxation and concentration. As Graham Jones also works with

British javelin record-holder, Steve Backley, someone has remarked that at least it should help her to throw the racket further, if nothing else!

Already the benefit is being seen in her game. Other players have remarked, "What's wrong with Lisa? She should be shouting and screaming." Even in the match where she lost to Robin Lambourne in the 1990 World Championship, she was in control of herself throughout.

As Lisa puts it "Graham has taught me breathing techniques for controlling panic and relaxation triggers to deal with anxiety".

Assessing her own progress during this period, Lisa commented, "Life on the squash court can be tough but since I became a Christian losing a match isn't the be-all and end-all." She quotes Paul's words to sum up her current motivation: "Do you not know that in a race all the runners run but only one gets the prize. Everyone who competes in the games goes into strict training. They do it to get a crown that will not last; but we do it to get a crown that will last forever."

Summing up Lisa's achievements is not easy. On the one hand her record speaks for itself – ranked two in the world for several years, four times finalist in the British Open, four times national champion, twice finalist in the World Open, tournament wins in Singapore, Malaysia, Finland, Canada, Ireland, etc. In Alex Cowie's words, she is "without question the best woman squash player in the world. She is more skilful than anyone and can do things with the racket that no other player can."

From another perspective, she could be seen as "always the bridesmaid, never the bride", that she has never quite fulfilled the potential she showed in the early eighties. She has been said to lack the "bloody-minded mental toughness" required to make it right to the top.

However, all in all, there is a strong case for believing

that the best of Lisa Opie is still to come. Her win in the 1991 British Open can be seen as evidence of this as can her increasing self-control and calmer manner on court. She would attribute this both to the influence of the sports psychologist, Graham Jones, who has helped her to relax on court, and a maturing Christian faith.

CAREER SUMMARY

Wins

1981	Junior World Championship
	British National Champion
1983	British National Champion
	British Under-23 Champion
1984	European Champion of Champions
	British Closed Championship
1985	Finnish Open
1986	Finnish Open
	Malaysian Open
	Australian Open
	New York Open
	British National Champion
1987	Finnish Open
	British National Championship
	European Champion of Champions
	Australian Open
	Irish Open
1988	Malaysian Open
	Irish Open
	Canadian Open
	Singapore Open
	New York Open
1989	Judy Travis International, Toronto
	Singapore Open
	New York Open
1990	Malaysian Open
	Singapore Open
1991	British Open
	Portuguese Open

Other

Runner-up in World Championship (1985 and 1987)
Runner-up in British Open (1982, 1983, 1984, 1986)

International

Over 50 appearances for England
Member of World Championship winning team, 1985, 1987, 1989, 1990

WILF SLACK

At first sight you might think it absurd to describe Wilf Slack as "a winner". He was born on the island of St Vincent in December 1954 and died in the Gambia in January 1989. His marriage in the mid-1980s ended in divorce and heartbreak. He had no children. He was a professional cricketer who played just three times for his country, and never established himself as a Test player. For most of his life he worried about the crucial relationships in his life. He was desperately lacking in confidence and could be diffident to the point of insecurity.

Yet Wilf was certainly a winner. Soon after his death his sister Phyllis and cricket journalist Bridgette Lawrence put together "an Appreciation" to which I am indebted for a number of quotes in this chapter. Those who knew Wilf best knew him as a winner.

Mike Brearley, England and Middlesex captain, wrote, "He was the sort of person who gave Christianity a good name."

West Indian opener, Desmond Haynes, who was signed as his replacement for Middlesex: "As everyone will tell you, he was a lovely guy."

Graham Barlow, his opening colleague in Middlesex's successful team of the 1980s, and someone who will feature regularly in this story: "Wilf was a living example of how to be a Christian . . . he accorded his fellow human beings respect and was one of the few people I knew who practised genuine humility."

Ian Botham, one of the greatest all-round cricketers to play the game: "I will always remember him as 'Bishop Tutu' (the nickname he acquired in the England team) . . . he was the most caring, genuine, happy, smiling cricketer."

Essex and England opening bowler Neil Foster: "The thing that always struck me was how calm he always seemed."

Former West Indies captain, Clive Lloyd: "I had great respect for him as a person and a professional."

England opening bowler Neil Williams: "He was like a big brother to me – a true gentleman, a genuine sort of person and the ideal team man."

An anonymous 13-year-old boy from Yorkshire wrote, "His cruelly untimely death has robbed the game he graced of one of its most naturally noble ambassadors . . . His example will shine longer and brighter than any dozen of the garish stars who overshadowed him in life."

Oh yes, Wilf was a winner.

Some time during the autumn of 1988 I suggested to him that he might like to go to the Gambia with the Cavaliers – a team of club cricketers organised by my cousin Michael Wingfield Digby. He had jumped at the idea. His days of touring with England were over and his repeated blackouts made long tours difficult. Short forays, especially to his beloved Africa, were very appealing.

Michael remembers how quickly Wilf became one of the team. "He took charge of a practice session in his usual unobtrusive way, introducing the party to beach cricket as there were no nets available. In the first one day match Wilf played well for 38, hitting a succession of sizzling boundaries . . . then he was given out LBW. He just gave a wry smile, although a lot of professionals would not have taken it so well."

He batted spendidly for an unbeaten 100 in the second match. After retiring to give others a knock he returned to the pavilion, and was surrounded by a crowd of shouting youngsters, "Practice, Mr Wilf, practice." Wilf could never resist children, so despite exhaustion and great heat he spent a long time playing with them.

The next game was the first "Test". The Gambians did well, scoring 248 despite two electrifying slip catches by Slack. Unfortunately he was then clean bowled for three, and by "stumps" the visitors were 78 for 8 and facing disaster.

Next day was Sunday. Wilf, Michael and some other members of the team went to the Cathedral for the morning service. Michael was worried that the two remaining wickets would fall and Wilf would not be there to open the innings second time round. "Don't flap, Wingers," Wilf said as they walked across to the ground. The follow-on duly came, and Wilf began fluently. He had got to 35 when he collapsed going for an easy second run. A doctor arrived within a few minutes but nothing could be done. It seems that Wilf suffered a massive heart attack and died very quickly. As Bridgette Lawrence wrote, "And so he died, as he may have wished, with the sun on his back and runs to his name. The timing was out, but the setting was perfect."

Phyllis asked me to speak at his funeral in London a couple of weeks later. For some time she had been attending the Kensington Temple in Notting Hill with Wilf. They both loved the lively services, the pulsating music and homespun humour of the Pastor, Wynne Lewis. Phyllis knew that Wilf would want the service to be at K.T., as people call it. A vast throng which included many England and County cricketers packed into the church. Mike Gatting, Wilf's Middlesex captain, spoke warmly and movingly of his long-time team mate:

"Wilfie was someone we all admired from afar and close up, such was his personality . . . He was a strong man who would listen to others' troubles but keep his own to himself." He concluded in a faltering voice, speaking of how every cricket player and supporter of the land felt, "Wilfie, we'll never forget you."

Of course, when someone dies there is a tendency to exaggerate their merits. This is especially so when the death is unexpected and premature. But no one who reads Bridgette Lawrence's appreciation, nor anyone who attended that funeral celebration, nor indeed anyone who knew Wilf Slack, could deny that all the things said about him then and subsequently are true. As Mike Selvey wrote, "He was a lovely, lovely man."

Wilf's first years were spent in relative poverty, in the hillside village of Troumaca in the Leeward part of the West Indies island of St Vincent. Phyllis was two years younger than Wilf, but their deep friendsh p was forged in their early years in the Caribbean. Like many West Indians the Slacks lived in an extended family. Mostly they were looked after by Aunt Yvonne and their grandfather, as both parents were busy working. By the time he was 12 and set off with Phyllis to join his parents who had moved to England, Wilf was emerging as a keen sportsman with all-round ability, especially at cricket. They did not use very sophisticated equipment in those early days – bread fruit, lemons and limes for balls, and coconut branches for bats.

Those early years on St Vincent left an indelible mark on Wilf's character. Years later his batting would be described as "more English than West Indian", but his personality was grafted in the West Indies. He would always appear laid back and carefree (although often he wasn't). Like many West Indians he would always find time for a sleep in the changing room. He loved to practise with children whenever he could, just as he had learnt the game himself "back home".

It was also a God-fearing house in which he lived and the Christian faith was taught him from the cradle. He never abandoned this faith, though probably only in the last few years of his life did it really blossom into a personal commitment to Jesus Christ.

In 1966 Phyllis and Wilf made the journey to England, like so many others, and joined their parents in the alien world of High Wycombe. They hardly knew their mother and father, and had never met their two brothers, Jeff and William. It was bleak and cold and they took a long time to adjust. But Wilf had his sport, at which he thrived, and he soon developed into an outstanding runner, holding the Buckinghamshire record for 440 and 880 yards, footballer and basketball player.

But cricket was number one. His background is unusual for a Test player. He began as a village cricketer. From the age of 14 to 19 he was the mainstay of the batting at Freith Cricket Club. Initially, he was all Caribbean flamboyance, but being promoted to opener settled him down, and he was canny enough to work out that if he mixed defence with attack he would occupy the crease for longer. Throughout his career Wilf loved to bat. He enjoyed it most in the middle but if that was impossible he would find a net and some bowlers somewhere. I vividly remember one wet day at Lords soon after his blackouts began. It was a dismal day and most of the players were curled up in a corner reading, or sitting about playing bridge and backgammon. There was no sign of Wilf in the changing room.

"Try the indoor school," suggested coach Don Bennett.

And sure enough Simon Hughes had been recruited for a long bowl at the Middlesex left-hander. We chatted for a while and he talked about the frightening faints that had begun to plague him.

"Maybe I should stop playing, Wingers," he said, "but I love to bat; to be honest I'd sooner go on playing, doing what I'm good at . . . and take what comes."

From Freith he moved to High Wycombe Cricket Club, and a higher standard of club cricket. But he did not forget his roots or his friends. In 1977 he wrote in the *Village Cricket Annual* of his days at Freith, "Two important lessons I learnt in those days were always to set your standards high and, most important, to enjoy your cricket. Cricket is a game to be played positively and enjoyed, whilst building firm friendships."

High Wycombe was one of several vital stepping stones into professional cricket. He did well for the club in 1975 (scoring over 1,000 runs) and went on a tour of Kenya – his first visit to Africa. He was a great success with everyone. Alan Juster, who played in the same side and was a close friend, comments, "They treated him like a black god." He was to visit Kenya twice more in 1974 and 1987; on each occasion he became more and more determined to help the youngsters to develop their cricketing skills. Kenau Barlow, Graham's wife, recalls him telling her quietly that he had a great passion: "I have something that is very important that I want to do one day . . . I want to teach the black children of Africa how to play cricket, how to play cricket the right way . . . that's what I really want to do."

In 1976 he played for Buckinghamshire in the Minor County Championship, and did sufficiently well to be picked by Don Bennett for the Middlesex Under-25's. Now a career in professional cricket was a real possibility. But he was old to be starting such a career, and there are always numerous young players who score thousands of runs in club cricket but cannot make the grade in first class. This is true, in fact, in every sport. For everyone who makes it to the top, like the people featured in this book, there are many more who fall by the wayside.

In 1976 most people would have said that that was the most likely fate for Slack. His left-handed style was a little awkward, and though a useful seam bowler he would never make a genuine all-rounder. His personality was not pushy or flashy, and he was not instantly noticeable in a crowd. In fact, in cricketing terms he did not exude "class". There were plenty around who did – Mike Gatting, Ian Gould, Graham Barlow and fellow West Indians Larry Gomes and Roland Butcher were all starting at Middlesex at this time. When you consider that these five batsmen (though, of course, Gould also kept wicket) as well as bowlers like Edmonds, Emburey, Selvey and Daniel all went on to play Test cricket, it is eary to see how the High Wycombe opener from St Vincent was somewhat overawed.

His first under-25s game was against Kent at Blackheath. Kent made about 180 or so, and Don Bennett told Wilf at tea that he would like him to open the innings. "He looked rather surprised and said that he thought some of the others should go in before him." In fact, he made a solid half-century and was on his way.

By this time Slack was a qualified electronics engineer with a decent job in High Wycombe. It was a big decision to abandon that career for the far-from-certain world of professional sport. But in 1977 the offer of a contract came and after a lot of heart-searching and seeking of advice from friends he decided to "give it a go". For the rest of his life Wilf was a 12-months-a-year professional cricketer.

For a few years he struggled to establish a place in an immensely strong Middlesex side. This was the "Brearley era". The former Cambridge captain had an almost guru-like reputation in the game. He was highly intelligent and articulate, a gifted leader, a proponent of the "inner game" and a meticulous analyser of every member of his team. Though Wilf had great respect for him, there is no doubt that he was also inhibited by his presence. Brearley himself acknowledges this: "It became clear to me for the first time, not only that Wilf had done less well while opening with me, but also that he felt that every time he played a loose shot this grey-headed old geezer down the other end would give a visible wince."

Brearley also has a shrewd assessment of Slack's batting technique: "He was one of the best players of genuinely fast bowling I have seen, bar none. For this he needed courage, of course. He also had a great technique against speed, standing up high to play down the lifting ball, never taking his eye off the ball even when he had to evade it hurriedly at the last moment. He was also basically a forward player, and was able to move on to the front foot, and not get too far back, even against the quickest bowling."

It is not entirely surprising that Slack established himself in the County side only when Brearley was selected to take over the England captaincy from Ian Botham during the Ashes series against Australia in 1981. So sensational were Botham's deeds for England in the games that followed that the almost equally remarkable batting of Wilf Slack for Middlesex was easily overlooked.

He had become a consistent scorer in the second eleven but his infrequent appearances in the County side had not been marked by success. In 1980 he scored prolifically in the second eleven championship, but had still not made a first class hundred when he was drafted into the team to play Kent at Lords. He opened the innings with Graham Barlow for the first time – both left-handers – though Barlow's flashing style contrasted sharply with Slack's more defensive game. A partnership of 367 for the first wicket established a Middlesex record, and Slack headed back for the pavilion with 181 to his name while Barlow had accumulated 174. He had already made 56 in the first innings so it looked as if a good run of form was beginning.

And so it was. In the next game he got 248 not out against Worcestershire, the highest score by a Middlesex player since Denis Compton's 252 not out against Somerset in 1948. In the next month, while Botham tamed the Australians, Slack scored 1,011 runs in 12 innings and won his County cap. He ended the season as the County's leading scorer and at the age of 27 had emerged from the shadows.

A number of factors combined to make it likely that Slack would eventually break through. Though always insecure about his ability ("You are only as good as your last innings," he would say), he thought hard about his game, and worked at his technique. He had improved steadily from 1977 to 1981. He was also using his winters wisely. In 1979–80 and 1980–81 he played club cricket for Ellerslie in Auckland, and was voted player of the year on both occasions. At the end of the 1980 season he also toured Zimbabwe with Middlesex and once again, feeling very much at home in Africa, did very well.

He had also found comfortable and welcoming "digs" with Beth Blik where he found a family atmosphere and a real "mother figure" in Beth. This was very important to the rather shy, gentle, retiring Slack. Previously he had shared a flat with Roland Butcher and intermittently with Wayne Daniel – an altogether more chaotic situation. Beth's daughters, Cornelia and Belisarius, spent hours with Wilf, laughing at and teasing him. He was wonderful with children. As Beth says, "I think we made a contribution to making him feel more relaxed."

The relationship with Graham Barlow was the icing on the cake. It is hard to imagine two more contrasting characters than Graham and Wilf. While Slack was calm, Barlow was frenetic; Slack was a peacemaker in the changing room, Barlow a trouble maker; Slack was a private man, Barlow shouted his situation from the rooftop. Slack's relationships tended to be deep and long lasting, Barlow's were complex and brief. Graham would later say that he came to see that Wilf's "understated approach to goodness was of the essence of what I needed in my life".

They were totally contrasting players as well. Though, as Brearley says, Wilf liked to come forward, Barlow sees him as predominantly a back foot player. This seeming contradiction is because of Slack's ability to "ride" the short pitched ball, getting up high with the weight on the back foot. In an era of short pitched bowling this has become a standard way of playing for openers.

Barlow was different. He needed to be forward, taking risks, looking to drive the ball whenever possible. Barlow was tremendously influenced by his feelings in those days, and very quickly he began to feel comfortable batting with Wilf. Between overs Barlow would be full of talk, bullying Wilf with advice and chiding him. It was water off a duck's back to the easy-going Vincentian, and just what they both needed. A tremendous bond was forged between them.

Strangely, it was not until 1986, right at the end of his career, that Barlow became a Christian. Wilf's gentle, consistent example was a major factor in Barlow's remarkable conversion. "Wilf gave me an example of how to lead a worthy life . . . he has given us a model to emulate," he wrote later.

In 1982 Slack opened the innings with Brearley and, overcoming his former nervousness, passed 1,000 runs for the second time. That was Brearley's last season and between 1983 and 1985 Barlow and Slack were undoubtedly the best opening partnership in the country. Slack developed his role as anchorman while the dashing Barlow would often catch the eye. I was a young clergyman in London in those days and would, as often as possible, nip down to Lords to see Middlesex bat and chat with the players in the changing room.

One of my last memories of Wilf will be watching him prepare to bat. He would be sitting quietly at the back of the changing room with his "coffin" – the case in which a cricketer keeps all his kit – neatly packed. He would be ready in good time, practising a few shots as the start of play approached. His appearance was immaculate. He was meticulously professional.

Meanwhile in the far corner Barlow would be engaged in frantic activity. His kit seemed to be all over the changing room and he would be chattering endlessly. "Andrew, nice to see you; anyone got my gloves? How's the church going? Not preaching too long? Have they gone? (referring to the umpires). Where the hell's my helmet?"

Wilf would be sitting quietly and if you caught his eye the big "watermelon grin" would spread across his face. He knew about Graham and he really like him.

These were the great years. Middlesex won the County Championship in 1982, came second in 1983, third in 1984, and won again in 1985. They were equally successful in one-day competitions, winning the Benson and Hedges in 1983 and the NatWest in 1984.

They were undoubtedly Slack's best years and it is tragic that his England career did not begin until his ill health was nearly upon him. One cannot help thinking that had he been picked for England in 1983 or 1984 he would have done his country proud.

In fact, at the end of 1985, he scored 201 not out for Middlesex against the Australians at Lords and was hopeful of selection for the tour of the Caribbean that winter. His season's aggregate of 1,618 runs at an average of nearly 50, and his proven record against fast bowling, of which there would be plenty in the West Indies, made him a red-hot tip for selection. Amazingly the selectors chose only two openers – Gooch and Robinson. It was particularly strange as Slack had been playing for the Windward Islands for two winters, 81–82 and 82–83, in the Shell Shield, and therefore knew both the opposition bowlers and the local conditions. He was terribly disappointed. "The Windward Islands had asked me to captain their Shell Shield side," he wrote in a newspaper article. "When I got 200 against the Aussies I had visions of the whole population crowding into Kingstown (the capital city of St Vincent) to see the local boy batting against the team he might have captained."

As a consolation he was chosen for the 'B' tour to Sri Lanka. This was a considerable challenge for Slack. When he began his first class career he had really struggled against spin bowling. In county cricket at that time there were very few high quality spinners and so it was not too much of a disadvantage, and anyway over the years Wilf had "netted" – practised – hard against Phil Edmonds and John Emburey, his Middlesex colleagues, who were probably the best spinners in English cricket at the time. Nevertheless, the leg spinners and left-armers of Sri Lanka were a real challenge. In six matches including four unofficial "Tests" he scored 431 runs and averaged 43.10.

England team in Trinidad and Tobago. Mike Gatting had been hit in the face by a ball from Malcolm Marshall and flown home. So Wilf's England career began with a duck in the first innings against Trinidad and Tobago! He got 37 in the second and that was enough to secure him selection for the Second Test in Port of Spain. Scores of 2 and 0 in that game, and another failure in the game against Barbados, meant he missed the Third and Fourth Tests. England were soundly thrashed in both games and again in the fifth, despite Slack's courageous 52 in the first innings.

He played just one more Test match scoring 0 and 19 in the Second Test at Headingley against India in 1986. Things went against him. He had been picked for the two One Day Internationals but had to withdraw because of injury. The Second Test came in the midst of a run of bad form. Later that year Graham Barlow was forced out of the game with a persistent back injury; the glory days were coming to an end. He still got his 1,000 runs for the season and was selected to tour Australia. This should have been the highlight of Wilf's cricket career but it turned into an anti-climax as he played only five matches on tour and was selected for none of the Test Matches or One Day Internationals.

His contribution off the field won him many friends. He was unfailingly enthusiastic and supportive, enjoying the success of the rest of the team. His Christian faith was becoming increasingly important to him at this time, and he would regularly disappear from the hotel to attend church or meet up with Christian friends. Botham and Allan Lamb nicknamed him "Bishop Tutu". Lamb recalls being in the sauna: "'Hey, Tutu,' said the white South African, 'chuck some more water on.' Quick as a flash he started running around after me, saying 'yes, sir, no sir,' and generally taking the mickey."

According to Simon Barnes writing in *The Times*, Wilf replied, "We are not in Johannesburg. Get your own water." Whichever way, it's a delightful story.

When things got a little heated or some teasing was going on, Wilf would say, "Hey, peace be with you, my brother." He drew high praise from Manager Micky Stewart: "Nobody has done more for team spirit than Wilf Slack, who, though not in the team, has made a great contribution backstage."

Wilf's last two seasons with Middlesex – 1987 and 1988 – involved new partnerships, first with Andy Miller and finally John Carr. He scored 1,419 runs in the Championship in 1987 despite an ongoing battle with the shoulder injury. That winter he visited New Zealand for the last time and played for Parnell in Auckland. The club asked him to introduce coaching programmes for the youngsters. He approach it with great enthusiasm and had groups of all ages from seven to twenty. Everybody warmed to his easy-going charisma.

In 1988 he batted beautifully, but ominously the fainting fits became more regular. Jim Davis, the Middlesex physio, was getting increasingly concerned. "No one could pinpoint the exact problem because there was no consistency in his attacks . . . He would go down . . . when there was no pressure on him, so it was impossible to tell when it would happen."

It happened finally on that hot, sad Sunday in Banjul. We all assembled at the Kensington Temple for the funeral. After the eulogies and the sermon, the coffin containing his body was opened. This is a Caribbean tradition giving friends and family a chance to pay their last respects. Wilf looked quite at peace in his England touring tie and blazer, his helmet and bat beside him. One by one the great assembly of those who esteemed him very highly filed past.

"Do not think that this is Wilfred you are looking at," called out Pastor Wynne Lewis. "It is just the house in which he used to live. Wilfred is with Jesus."

CAREER SUMMARY compiled by Eddie Solomon

Batting	M	Inn	NO	Runs	HS
Middlesex					
First Class	210	348	8	12,565	248*
Sunday League/Cup	104	96	13	2,360	101*
Gillette/NatWest	26	26	1	820	98
Benson & Hedges	36	36	4	895	110
Second XI	51	88	6	3,250	202*
Under-25s	22	22	3	803	80
Windward Islands					
First Class	9	17	1	585	97
England					
Test Matches	3	6	0	81	52
Other First Class	15	27	1	719	96
*All First Class Matches**	237	398	40	13,950	248*

Bowling	Overs	Maidens
First Class	229	59
Sunday League/Cup	176.4	1
Gillette/NatWest	84	6
Benson & Hedges	7	0
Second XI	69	18
Under-25s	43.2	2
Other First Class		

All First Class Matches

*He passed 1,000 first class runs in a season eight times.

CAREER SUMMARY

Average	CT	50s	100s	Boundaries (Fours/ Sixes)	Runs per 100 Balls
40.53	144	66	25	1,282/33	48.38
28.43	20	16	1	163/8	60.90
32.80	4	7	0	84/2	56.12
27.96	5	5	1	76/4	48.48
39.63	39	21	5	410/17	46.88
42.26	6	7	0	80/8	59.00
36.56	10	3	0		
13.50	3	1	0		
27.65	17	5	0		
38.96	174	75	25		

Runs	Wickets	Average	Best Bowling
632	19	33.26	3–17
878	34	25.82	5–32
317	8	39.62	3–57
34	0	–	0–6
162	9	18.00	2–3
186	5	37.20	2–32
56	2	28.00	
688	21	32.76	3–17

CONCLUSION

All the people featured in this book have in common that they are Christians in sport. The possible exception is Wilf Slack, but we like to think that he is opening the batting in heaven with Jack Hobbs!

They are sportspeople who have competed at the highest level in their chosen sport and have found a Christian faith entirely relevant. All of them have found that winning is not enough.

The authors of this book are respectively the General Director and the Management and Finance Director of Christians in Sport. It is their full-time employment. Andrew is an ordained Anglican minister attached to St Aldates, a large city centre church in Oxford, while Stuart, with a working background in public administration, is a member of Northwood Hills Evangelical Church. Other key leaders of Christians in Sport come from various Christian denominations.

Christians in Sport is about establishing a strong, vibrant, attractive Christian presence in the world of sport. Over the last fifteen years or so an increasing number of men and women in top level sports in Great Britain and elsewhere in the world have identified themselves as committed Christians. Some have been marvellously "converted" – for instance, Kriss Akabusi and Lisa Opie. Others, like Bernhard Langer or the Davies brothers, have found the confidence to express a faith which has always been a part of their lives.

Christians in sport, through its small full-time staff and
growing army of volunteers, offers support for these
"public" Christians as they try to live in a Christian way
and influence their team mates and colleagues for Christ.
As a movement Christians in Sport is unashamedly
evangelisitic, longing that more and more people
throughout the world should stand up and be counted
for Jesus.

But the method employed to propagate the faith is not
insensitive Bible-bashing. Individual ministers – men
and women – work in particular sports as chaplains and
counsellors. They have often had experience themselves
as competitors in the world of sport and have received
training in sports ministry.

At the time of writing some 35 of the English Football
League clubs have appointed a local minister or vicar as
an honorary chaplain. In addition, pastors travel with the
tennis men's and women's teams, professional golf tours
and the track and field athletics circuit. Christians in
Sport staff are regularly involved in the official chap-
laincy to the world's major sports events – 1986 and 1990
Commonwealth Games, 1988 Olympic Games, 1991
World Student Games, etc.

The chaplains understand the seriousness of high-
level sport, the sacrifices required in order to succeed,
and they are aware of the problems that many sports-
people face.

Of course they long for people to come to know Christ
as those featured in this book have, but they are
also there to care as Jesus did when he was alive,
unconditionally and without strings attached.

Increasingly, administrators in sport are waking up to
the fact that people have been made physical, emotional
and spiritual beings. Great efforts have been made to
look after athletes physically. Doctors and physio-

therapists abound. The whole science of sports psychology is expanding as coaches explore ways of motivating their athletes. But the essence of the "person", his spiritual wellbeing, has been largely ignored until now. It is the experience of those whose lives are described in this book that they have only known "wholeness" of life since they became spiritually alive. This is the gift of God in Jesus to all who believe.

Christians in Sport is not only about famous people! There is a great concern for sport and recreation at every level. Local churches are being encouraged to involve their local community in sports as a halfway house to church membership. Christians in Sport has helpful literature on how churches can do this. Through a local group structure "ordinary" sports people at club and college level are being encouraged to see their ability at and interest in sport as a gift from God which gives them access to a world which needs to hear of His love.

Even the armchair enthusiast is not forgotten. Perhaps the main reason why there has been such an increase in the numbers of professing Christians playing sport in recent years is that more and more people are praying for the world of sport, that God's Kingdom, the influence of Jesus, would be known more and more.

So wherever you are you can be involved in this exciting ministry. If you write to:

      Christians in Sport,
      PO Box 93,
      Oxford,
      OX2 7YP

Andrew or Stuart would be delighted to tell you more.

BIBLIOGRAPHY

Readers who wish to find out more about the sports-people featurd in this book may be interested in the following:

Kriss Akabusi
Kriss Akabusi on Track by Ted Harrison, Lion, October 1991

Kitrina Douglas
"Women in Sport" by Kitrina Douglas in *Women to Women*, edited by Kathy Keay, MARC/Evangelical Alliance, 1988

Alan Knott
It's Knott Cricket by Alan Knott (autobiography), Macmillan 1985
Cricketing Legends – Alan Knott, a BBC Sports Video, BBC 1990

Bernhard Langer
While the Iron Is Hot by Bernhard Langer (autobiography), Stanley Paul 1988

Wilf Slack
Wilf Slack: An Appreciation by Bridgette Lawrence, A & N Moghul 1989

General
A Loud Appeal by Andrew Wingfield Digby, Hodder & Stoughton 1988

A Whole New Ball Game by Gerald Williams, Marshall Pickering 1983 (several subsequent reprints)

Winners Every Time, a video by Christians in Sport 1988

The Flying Scotsman (a biography of Eric Liddell) by Sally Magnusson, Quartet Books, London 1981

On The Right Track by John Searle, Marshall Pickering 1987